PRAISE FC

"If you are feeling overwhelmed by how to master your finances in an age where data is plentiful but true advice is scarce, read this book."

—**Ivan R. Misner, PhD,** Founder of BNI and
New York Times Bestselling Author

"Rassman has a unique and insightful way of viewing the financial world that shouldn't be missed. The future is now and Rassman gives the tools to navigate it."

—**Jake Pfeiffer,** JD, Campbell Tax Law

"*Atlas Shift* is an authentic, no-nonsense resource for today's financial world. Rassman's refreshing insights and actionable advice make this book the perfect guide to taking ownership of your finances once and for all."

—**Lynn Swords,** Founder, Ink & Key

"Using philosophy, history, economics, and a background in personal finance, Rassman brings forth a new vision and unsuspected dimensions of an industry resistant to change."

—**Laurel Rosen,** President/CEO,
Santa Monica Chamber of Commerce

"This is the book that, 5-10 years from now, most investors will wish they had read. In a clear and concise manner, Rassman analyses the systemic problems within the financial planning universe and the reasons why consumers owe it to themselves to expect more. If you have financial goals that you take seriously, do yourself and your family a favor and read *Atlas Shift.*"

—**Justin Pfeiffer,** President, Max Cap Financial

"This book is useful for the lay person who wants concrete guidance on selecting the right financial manager. Valuable insight is provided, too, through an education in the history of the industry alongside a sharp critique of its current practices and the crucial need for reform and modernization."

—**Jay Levin,** Founder, *LA Weekly*

ATLAS SHIFT

ATLAS SHIFT

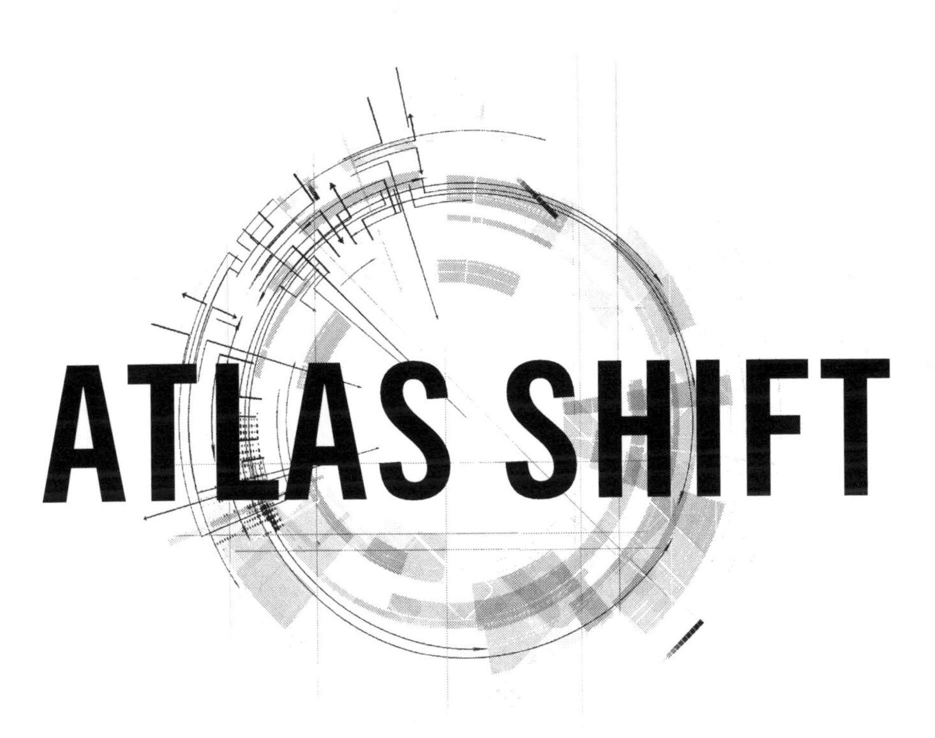

MASTERING YOUR FINANCIAL EXPERIENCE IN THE POST-INFORMATION AGE

WILLIAM RASSMAN

Aught & Wreath Publishing

First published by Aught & Wreath Publishing

First Edition

Centric Capital Advisors, LLC
12424 Wilshire Blvd., 9th Floor
Los Angeles, CA 90025
(310) 579-9060
info@atlasshift.com
www.atlas-shift.com

Library of Congress Control Number: 2018960814
Paperback: 978-0-9978023-4-4
eBook: 978-0-9978023-3-7

To Mom and Dad—

Thank you for believing in me, especially when I didn't.

Table of Contents

INTRODUCTION

The Future of Your Money

There's nothing like the crunch of the ice under your skates as you make that first hard turn on a frigid winter day. I can close my eyes and feel that sensation in my feet even though I traded my skates for a pair of oxfords long ago. Like many throughout the United States, Canada, Scandinavia, and other hotbeds of hockey fandom, I spent hours upon hours on the ice growing up.

Fans of hockey, readers of business magazines, and attendees of seminars and conferences have no doubt heard a famous quote often attributed to hockey legend Wayne Gretzky: "Skate to where the puck is going to be, not where it has been." I have studied the game extensively and skated with some pretty darn good hockey players who had what is called good “hockey sense.” *Hockey sense* is commonly used to describe the instincts of a player who appears to anticipate what is about to happen on the ice and then reacts a bit sooner than the other players. Terms like *sees the ice well* and *great anticipation* are also used when recounting these players’ skills. Players who demonstrate hockey sense typically possess individual skills that are superior to those of their teammates or opponents. They dazzle the fans with their quick sticks, maneuvers, and overall abilities. They always seem to be in the right place at the right time.

The wisdom we needed to get to today is no longer the wisdom we need to take us into the future.

My goal in writing this book is to help you sharpen and apply your own anticipatory hockey sense when managing your investments in a swiftly changing world. The wisdom we needed to get to today is no longer the wisdom we need to take us into the future, and I don’t want you left waiting for a puck that never comes. I am a futurist by nature, so I am going to give you some key tools and insights that will help you anticipate where the puck is going, so you know where to be to capitalize on its movement.

I am also an older millennial who has worked in the financial services industry for the better part of a decade, which means I have enough experience to understand how the industry works while having a completely different interpretation, approach, and outlook than the silver-haired partners of most brokerage and advisory firms. To be clear, this book is meant to strengthen your common sense, not to substitute for it. It is also not a substitute for the advice of your personal or professional advisors. It is meant to give you an education, a wealth of knowledge, and a background that will inform your perception and outlook.

THE FUTURE IS WAITING

The advice to anticipate where the puck is going rings especially true in today's era of big data, which is expanding every day. Data is the world's most potent, flourishing unnatural resource. This resource is inherently predictive; in other words, we have the potential to use it to see where the puck is going. In fact, we've entered the golden age of data-based prediction, where the patterns of the past provide a hint of what's to come in the future. A frenzy of number crunching leads to valuable and sometimes surprising insights.

The takeaway? Focus on the present or past—where the puck was—and you're sure to fall behind. Focus on the future—where the puck is going to be—and you're setting yourself up to remain ahead of the curve.

I am particularly partial to the importance of anticipating the future because of an epiphany I had toward the beginning of my career, when I had the opportunity to work at a branch of a financial services company with a highly successful woman. A vice president in a firm with hundreds of millions of dollars under management, she carefully selected interns and junior brokers from Ivy League schools to work in the firm's hallowed halls. Naturally, I was both impressed and intimidated by her. One day, during a difficult day for the market, I summoned my courage and asked her what she was telling her clients.

"The market goes up; the market goes down," she replied before turning away.

I stood there, looking after her as she walked with brisk, confident steps into her office. One thought clung to my mind, and try as I could, I wasn't able to get rid of it.

With all your experience and education, that is the best you can come up with?

I will never know what her reaction would have been if I had asked her this question. But one thing was clear: she was overleveraging the trust clients placed in her. She clearly wasn't operating from the Gretzky School of Management. These types of advisors aren't on the ice with the rest of us; they couldn't care less where the puck is. They're up in the stands, eating a hot dog, watching everything unfold just like you are. They don't know what's coming, because they're not trying to get ahead of it.

The game has changed, my friends. I call it the *atlas shift*, the moment that the map of financial services has veered away from what it used to be. The industry's crust has broken open and the plates beneath it have moved. It's hard to anticipate where the puck is going when the ice is undulating under your skates and you're just trying to stay upright.

Let me put any initial worries you may have to rest, as best as I can. I provide a framework in this book that defines the new landscape after the atlas shift that many of us may not even have realized has already occurred. This shift has taken us from the Information Age to what I call the *Specialization Age,* and it has disrupted countless industries: transportation, hospitality, merchandising, and publishing, to name a few. The landscape of the financial services industry is shifting, too, and although clients are begging for the old way of doing things to be disrupted, the industry itself is slow to respond.

Financial advisors who catch on to this demand for a new kind of service and who move to meet it will be able to grow their company's market share and deliver twenty-first-century-worthy service to clients. The self-empowered client who gravitates toward this new kind of advisor—an *atlas** *client*—will receive the support and guidance needed to live a life of well-being and financial security.

---

* In Greek mythology, Atlas was a Titan assigned the responsibility of holding up the sky or, in some accounts, the pillars that separate the earth and the sky.[1]

This book is also designed to help you develop your own intuition and skill set when it comes to managing your investments in today's unique and fast-changing world of the Specialization Age. I want to empower you to make your own atlas shift from the Information Age to the Specialization Age when it comes to managing your money so you can meet your financial goals and experience life as you want it to be. As the rules of the Specialization Age come into focus, the rules that guide how we manage our money need to be brought into focus, too. Have you and your financial advisor kept up?

I want you to be able to identify the right kind of advisor for you in this new age, and I want you to have the insight you need to take a hands-on role in managing your money with the support of this advisor. With this book, I will reduce some of the overwhelming nature of your task, which has been exacerbated by the information overload of the Specialization Age, so you can reengage your finances in the modern world.

CONCLUSION: WINNERS AND LOSERS

I am often asked why I wrote this book. In response, I invite the person asking the question to take that one step further and ask, Why am I the right person to write this book? Maybe it is because I have significant experience in investing and a nontraditional view of it because of the timing of my entry into the industry. Maybe it's because defiance runs deep within me and I loathe authority. Maybe it's because I love being an innovator and not a duplicator; I'm much too competitive to be the latter. In truth, it is a mix of all of the above.

I grew up in a financial services environment. My father held the position of marketing manager for First Financial Bank in Stevens Point, Wisconsin. Not to brag, but I was the star of their holiday marketing campaign. Yet life as a toddler model was just as glamorous as it sounds, from what I remember. Even at a young age, I remember being keenly aware of what my father did and the ways in which he did it. Marketing for a bank, after all, is selling in a service-oriented industry and hence should center around pitching services that satisfy the customers' needs. This gave me the framework for understanding how people choose to allocate their dollars and how they form money-centric relationships. After all, is that not what financial services boil down to? Choosing a financial services provider is all about finding the person or shop you think is the best fit to help you with your money.

When I grew up, it felt natural to start my own career in financial services. In May 2008, after I had some college classes under my belt, I started work as a summer intern at a large investment firm in the Financial District of New York City. With a few suits my dad helped me pick out and a shiny new briefcase, I was ready to take on the world, or so I thought.

Students of the market who are familiar with the financial crisis of 2007–2008 will remember that in May 2008, the Dow Jones Industrial Average had managed to rise above 13,000 after months of struggle, and it seemed the worst of the subprime mortgage crisis was over. No such luck. As anyone who's read, seen, or heard of *The Big Short* knows, a house of cards built by Wall Street traders—who packaged subprime home mortgage loans into collateralized debt obligations (Know what those are? Neither did anyone else), won them top scores from ratings agencies, and sold them to banks and other investors—tumbled in 2008, taking Lehman Brothers, plenty of investors, and the Dow's daily average with it. This set off the financial crisis of 2007–2008, which required years to recover from. By July 2008, the crisis had spread even to the government-sponsored agencies Fannie Mae and Freddie Mac, leaving them in dire need of a government bailout. The

Treasury Department guaranteed $25 billion of their loans and bought shares of Fannie's and Freddie's stock. The Federal Housing Administration insured $300 billion in new loans. The Dow fell again, closing at 10,962.54 on July 15. It rebounded and remained above 11,000 for the rest of the summer.

Do you want to build on lessons learned and get ahead of the curve, or do you want to stay in your comfort zone?

It was quite an introduction to Wall Street. During this time, I was cold-calling executives and opening my pitch with the question, "What approach are you taking with your investments?" I was ridiculous, and I would have hung up on me if I were at the receiving end of the call. On the bright side, I did get many leads and considered it a successful summer. Most important, I saw firsthand the type of devastation a market dislocation brings, on top of being keenly aware, via my recent economics courses, that there is a winner and a loser on every trade. My learning about financial management had truly begun, and real life, complete with its real consequences, was the teacher. I share some key lessons from my real-world education in this book:

- how to free financial advisors so they can be true fiduciaries
- how technology both helps and hinders in financial matters
- the importance of true diversification of assets
- the elements of a comprehensive wealth management plan

You may well be asking yourself, Why do I need to learn my own lessons on financial management now? You do not. No one does. But you do have a choice: Do you want to build on lessons learned and get ahead of the curve, or do you want to stay in your comfort zone and feel the intensity of the pains of a delayed change later? What is clear is that the financial landscape is changing, so there may be fewer and fewer cozy corners in which to hide. I myself am a proponent of making change proactively rather than reactively. That is why I wrote this book, to empower you and other atlas clients who are ready to take responsibility and create meaningful new partnerships.

As a CERTIFIED FINANCIAL PLANNER™ (CFP®) with a head for deep thinking, a passion to revolutionize financial management, and a desire to empower today's engaged investors, I could spend a lifetime exploring these topics. For now, let's spend the next nine chapters on them, together. Join me on the journey to acquire the updated map for financial services in the twenty-first century.

DEFINITION OF *ATLAS*[2]

1 *capitalized* : a Titan who for his part in the Titans' revolt against the gods is forced by Zeus to support the heavens on his shoulders

2 *capitalized* : one who bears a heavy burden

3 a : a bound collection of maps often including illustrations, informative tables, or textual matter

b : a bound collection of tables, charts, or plates

4 the first vertebra of the neck

5 *plural usually* **atlantes**: a male figure used like a caryatid as a supporting column or pilaster

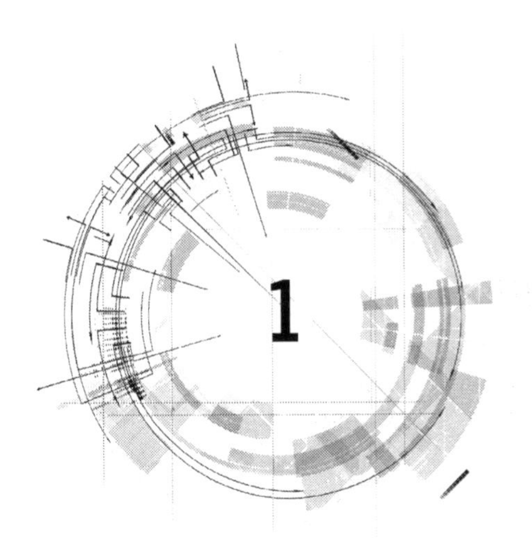

1

Tracing the Turns: How We Got Here

We've all heard of the Information Age. It's the era of the Internet, email, big data, and cable news networks delivering news twenty-four hours a day. The fundamentals of the Information Age are still everywhere—computers, the Internet, fiber-optic cables, microprocessors, 4G, and 4K. Yet, if we look more closely, it becomes apparent that the waves of information pouring out of the Information Age have forced us into a new era, where we must specialize to be able to manage it all. I call this new time the *Specialization Age*.

Is the Information Age over? No, I am not saying it is dead. How could I, with technology penetrating further into our lives, our work, and our homes every day? What I am saying is that the Information Age has shifted, become more nuanced, and funneled itself naturally into its next rendition. Call it the Information Age 2.0 or the Specialization Age, as I do in this book. Whatever you call it, take from this discussion the notion that we are in a new time. Consider the following examples of the transition from information to specialization to shed further light on the topic.

The Information Age has flooded our feeds with more news than we can possibly read; the Specialization Age has given us news aggregators like AP Mobile, Pocket and Flipboard to curate news stories for us. The Information Age made us busier at work handling emails, online conferencing, and data flow; because we are so busy working longer hours, the Specialization Age sends dinner ingredients to our door á la companies like HelloFresh and BlueApron because we don't have time to plan our own meals and grocery shop. Even entertainment has become specialized. While the Information Age gave us Netflix DVDs delivered to our door for family movie night, the Specialization Age gives us digital Netflix movies delivered to our individual devices so that each member of the family can watch something different while sitting on the same couch.

Why should we care about the Specialization Age in a book about mastering your financial experience? Because to develop this mastery, we must shift from the financial-information overload of the Information Age. That overload, which is prone to sinking many of us, stands in stark contrast to the customized financial experience which provides us a buoy. We need to find financial professionals who we can turn to for help in filtering and processing all the financial information available to us in the unique ways that we need it to meet our life goals.

While the Specialization Age has arrived in the realm of media, technology, and other industries like hospitality, retail, and publishing, the financial industry has remained largely stuck in the past. Whether due to inflexible structures, government regulation, a broken compensation system, or something else, this is problematic for consumers today for the many reasons to be explored in this book. Here's an overview of how I see traditional financial services of the past versus financial services of the future. If you read closely, you will be able to sense the problems of the past versus the benefits of the future.

Table 1.1: Financial Services: Past versus Future

PAST (20th Century & the Information Age)	FUTURE (21st Century: Information & Specialization Ages)
The financial industry is separated into distinct silos and there is no coordination among these professionals.	The financial experience advisor quarterbacks a team of professionals, coordinating your efforts to meet a holistic life plan.
Financial professionals sell you products and receive a commission on each sale.	The financial experience advisor provides you comprehensive guidance and receives compensation for time spent with you or as a percentage of your net worth.
Financial professionals sell you products that are suitable for you regardless of whether you really need them.	The financial experience advisor allows your unique needs to guide the advice they provide.
Financial advisors help you diversify your portfolio through a balanced mix of stocks and bonds that are expected to minimize pain felt from market dips in a less globalized world.	Financial experience advisors help you diversify your portfolio across *strategies*, as many stocks and bonds tend to react the same in a highly connected, globalized world.

Table 1.1 is not meant to disparage financial services of the past. This industry's emergence over the 20th century was a great stride forward for consumers, who now had professionals to help them invest, save, manage, and divest their money (see the Bonus Chapter at the end of this book for more on the history of wealth across the ages). As with all industries, however, there is value to progression; there is benefit to evolution. The Specialization Age offers us so many benefits in other industries; it's time for financial services to catch up.

A look at how we have shifted from Information to Specialization can increase our understanding of the Specialization Age—why it exists, what it offers, and what it requires, including in a financial context—so we can be prepared to seek and partner with advisors suited to meet our needs as consumers, today and in the future.

FROM INFORMATION TO SPECIALIZATION: HOW DID WE GET HERE?

In the early stages of the Information Age, technology ran relatively slowly. Users of the newfangled computer operating system Microsoft Windows 3.1 sat for seconds on end, watching the hourglass icon drip sand until the desired computer application would open. Turning on one's computer was an opportunity to run to the bathroom and take a coffee break or, if one was feeling particularly patriotic, to sing all the verses of *The Star-Spangled Banner*.

As the Information Age entered its heyday, computer processors started to move at light speed, and the MP3, first touted for its storage capability, allowed people to download music instantly or stream. AOL was no longer the only e-mail provider: we had Hotmail, Yahoo Mail, and then Gmail. Not only did traditional newspapers and television networks go virtual, but new online media emerged, like *The Huffington Post* and Twitter, adding more information to the cyber-ether.

At first, access to all this information was a boon for the consumer: now you could read the newspaper without spending a dollar or book a trip without using a travel agent. But as the Internet grew, so did the number of questions: Which online news publication should you follow? Should you book your next vacation using Kayak, TripAdvisor, or Expedia? With all this information came choice, and with choice came the need for specialization, because otherwise, on what basis could a choice be made? For example, travelers trying to select between travel websites might choose Kayak for the prices, TripAdvisor for the reviews, or Expedia for selection. In other words, consumers could only digest and use so much.

Technology proved overwhelming at times. Although most people wouldn't admit it, they carried a sense of guilt that they were falling behind on, well, everything. E-mails stacked up in in-boxes faster than they could be answered, links to great articles sent to them by friends and family members piled up without being visited, and episodes of their favorite TV shows filled the DVR to capacity so that the person who programmed the recording had no choice but to dedicate a whole weekend to binge-watching to catch up. Who had time to mow their own lawn or cook dinner? The faster people could access information, the busier they got. Everyone needed to learn how to prioritize, economize, and filter. They needed to become selective about what information they took in and hire specialists to help them manage it all.

FINANCIAL SERVICES, AT YOUR SERVICE

So what does a financial service look like in the Specialization Age? It is definitely multifaceted and holistic. Tomorrow's wealth has the potential to be more directed and connected, because the holder has a greater understanding of the impact of his assets. Atlas clients will see their wealth

- as something that they control and can use to better their lives
- as assets that they are assisted in managing by their financial experience advisor and his or her team, whom atlas clients have hired to ensure the wealth achieves the goals they have set for their holdings and themselves

- as a means in and of itself, via purposeful investment, of creating change for themselves, their families, and their communities.

In the Specialization Age, atlas clients have newfound transparency into their entire financial household via technology (fostered in the Information Age) as well as unfettered access to accomplish what they desire with their wealth—be it personal goals or broader changes. This comes through the assistance and shared responsibility of a *team* of experts all working towards these goals and changes. By being an active participant in this process, the atlas client is now in a supreme position to effect change in whatever arena he or she may wish to influence.

Although some will continue to measure the success of their wealth in decreasing fractions of time, others will consider exercising more patience. Given the increasing transparency enabled by the Information and Specialization Ages, trust between clients and financial advisors could grow; further, because the effects of their investments will be easier to monitor and verify, wealth holders will be able to have more confidence and even pride in how they allocate and use their assets. At the same time, we'll recognize that our true assets aren't just financial. Ideas and the specialization of skill will move everyone forward too.

In the Specialization Age, the legacy of the Information Age remains: firms will always need to harness information in practical ways. Just as most of them still need modern techniques to make their products cheaply, efficiently, and even more simply (a legacy of the Industrial Revolution), and just as the population needs an abundant supply of food to fuel (a legacy of the Agricultural Revolution) an industrial workforce, information will remain necessary but become insufficient to assure a firm's success. Talk of big data, for example, feels like an attempt to strain a few more drops of juice out of an already-squeezed orange, just as Six Sigma was a way of squeezing more value out of the

Industrial Revolution. Both are valuable concepts, but their benefits are incremental, not revolutionary. The big data craze seems to be an unintentional red herring. Many of the folks who are excited about this concept are also the people who have a vested interest in your believing the Information Age is still at its peak. This seemingly plausible but ultimately irrelevant diversionary tactic is throwing you off the trail. Today's most valuable commodity is attention.

MANAGING INFORMATION OVERLOAD THROUGH FOCUSED ATTENTION

So what are the consequences of a world that is experiencing too much information? It is not uncommon for a person doing research in an attempt to make an informed decision to be overwhelmed with the amount of available information and give up, making no decision at

COMMODITIES ACROSS THE AGES

The common thread between all historical ages is that there has always been a scramble to gain access to an era's most valuable commodity. Whereas today's most valued commodity, in my view, is attention, it was once food.

Food. In tribal times, from the beginning of human existence to about 10,000 BCE, the most valuable commodity was food. Every single day, nomadic tribes had to find enough food to feed the group, a struggle seemingly without end. Many tribes may have relocated only during the change of seasons, as different foods became available or, more to the point, unavailable.

Land. When we learned to farm, human beings leapt from a nomadic life (chasing the food) to the domestication of plants and animals (controlling the food) on a specific parcel of land. The transition to farming meant that people didn't have to hunt or scavenge. They now had the ability (to a degree, at least) to control availability. This is when land became the most valuable commodity and spanned the general time period from 10,000 BCE to the 1700s CE.

Farming had other effects on lifestyle and society. Because one farmer could produce enough food to feed several people, other people were freed from farming to act on their ideas, experiment, and discover new trades, vocations, and passions in the world around them. People could mine and find uses for natural metals, discover new medicines, focus on religious beliefs and worship, make pottery, provide security, or pursue other ideas and interests, such as building wealth. The extra food and free time from farming allowed for the division and diversification of labor and led to net gains for the larger society.

Capital. Next, in the late 1700s, came the Industrial Revolution, which ushered in game-changing technologies, new types of transportation, and a drastically different way of life for many. It lasted for over one hundred years, spreading during that time from Britain to the rest of Europe and the United States. At the beginning of the Industrial Revolution, plenty of people lived in cities, but a large number—many of them farmers—populated the countryside. When the manufacturing of goods moved from small shops and homes to large factories, so too did people move from rural areas to big cities to work.

The critical takeaway from this period is that the central, most valuable commodity shifted from land to capital, and the transition was made possible by ideas, the human innovations that created machines and invented efficiencies that society embraced and deployed. With advancements in industry, the more capital you had, the more products you could produce, whether it be cars, textiles, or telegraph machines.

Time. The Information Age started with the technological divide of the 1970s, where inventions like the microprocessor, the microcomputer, optical fiber, and TCP/IP protocol allowed people to store, process, and gain access to information more quickly than ever before. The Information Age brought with it new forms of entertainment, commerce, research, work, and communication. Apple, Twitter, Google, and all the other A-list companies of our time do one thing well: provide a service aimed at saving time. People use their iPhones because they can communicate faster; Elon Musk uses Twitter so he can inform all his followers simultaneously of the latest company news; Google searches the far reaches of the Internet for answers to the most complicated of queries.

Remember the adage "time is money"? That saying doesn't go nearly far enough. Time is not just the equivalent of currency: it defines the Information Age. Whether it is the latest stock prices, sports scores, or celebrity gossip, people want their information, and they want it now! This, in a sense, has warped our relationship with time. It used to take us forever to get information; now it takes virtually no time to track down more than you ever wanted to know. While more can often be done in less time in the Information Age than the Industrial Age, we now expect to accomplish more than we used to in any given period of time. Hey, if we can search up a pancake recipe on Google in five seconds, why can't we cook those pancakes just as fast? In the Information Age, we expect ourselves to get more done in less time, while bumping up against the human limitations of reality. While we'd expect technology to help us do our jobs faster—and sometimes it certainly does—it has largely increased the workload we are expected to accomplish. A testament to this are the following statistics:

- The average work week in 1890 was 100 hours/week.[1]
- The average work week in 1970 was 39 hours/week.[2]
- The average work week in 2018 was 44 hours/week.[3]

In the Information Age, time is the most valuable commodity.

Attention. Today, we are quick to access information we think will help us, but we cannot often make sense of it or use it appropriately. While most of us probably agree that access to information is good, it is not the be-all, end-all solution to today's challenges. As the founder of CD Baby Derek Sivers explained it, "If information were the answer, we'd all be billionaires with perfect abs."[4]

With multiple sources of stimulation available at our fingertips, the capacity to focus and concentrate on a particular activity is falling. A 2015 study by Microsoft indicated that the human attention span is now eight seconds, down from twelve seconds in 2000.[5] To put things in perspective: A goldfish has a nine-second attention span! Available in finite amount and sought after by many, attention is the central resource of the Specialization Age.

Table 1.2 provides an overview of the most valued commodities across the ages.

Table 1.2: Overview: Rassman Theory of Capitalistic Economic Evolution

Characteristic	Tribal Times	Agricultural Revolution	Industrial Revolution	Information Age	Specialization Age
Time Period	Beginning–10,000 BCE	10,000 BCE–1700s CE	1760–1920	1970s–20??	Now
Most Valuable Commodity	Food	Land	Capital	Time	Attention
Economic Backbone of Society	Hunting & Gathering	Farming	Manu-facturing	Services	Experiences
Foundational Currency	Ideas	Ideas	Ideas	Ideas	Ideas

Note: The foundational currency across the ages is always ideas, that is, the latest cutting-edge method for *X*. More and better ideas mean more and better innovation.

all. The tsunami of data forces us to realize that we cannot master the issue at hand, and we often end up falling back on a preexisting belief or cognitive biases for which our brains are wired.

Alternatively, some people engage in endless research, thinking that just one more click will reveal the ultimate informational source that will help them make the absolute best decision. In effect, they hamstring themselves, unable to move forward because they lack the willingness to choose a dependable enough source, make a decision, and progress.

Others think they are experts simply because they have access to information, not recognizing the value that professionals still bring to the table in helping us filter and make sense of the information. A little learning can be a dangerous thing. Doctors encounter this problem daily, as patients show up with an often incorrect self-diagnosis they found on the Internet.

For businesses, there is a significant consequence to this informational excess. Organizations must become masters of *attention management*—making sure that people are focused on the right set of issues and not distracted by the dozens of equally interesting issues that could also be discussed. The reality is that people tend to think in bits and bytes now. The attention span is down to approximately six hundred words on any given subject. Our minds tend to want "chunked" information rather than long lines of text. This has implications for how firms manage their internal processes, with much greater emphasis now being placed on holding people's attention. It also has massive consequences for how businesses manage their consumer relationships, as the traditional sources of "stickiness" in those relationships are being eroded.

Attention is a different kind of resource. You can't buy it, rent it, borrow it, store it, save it, renew it, or multiply it. All you can do is give it. There is no way you can save attention for future use, because all attention must be given now. Unlike other resources, such as time, talent, education, or money, we all have a very finite amount of attention. Unlike time, which will march on infinitely with or without us, our attention is a personal and finite resource.

Attention is a different kind of resource. You can't buy it, rent it, borrow it, store it, save it, renew it, or multiply it. All you can do is give it.

ATTENTION AND YOUR MONEY

This leads us to how we manage our attention when it comes to our money. I propose that your success and failure, in almost every part of your life, depends almost entirely on how you manage your attention. It's well worth your time and attention to understand how much attention you need to be putting toward your money and how to manage it.

Nowadays, it requires far less time and attention spent to have a solid understanding of your finances. So what once might have taken setting aside a couple hours to pull together statements and review far-flung accounts and policies can now take minutes. That decrease in attention required means more people can leverage said lesser attention to yield far greater understanding of their own finances. It is also important how attention is broken up. If you have a portal that lets you see a snapshot of your financial household that is updated everyday, you can more frequently check in to keep up to date.

CONCLUSION: A TIME FOR SHIFT

Albert Einstein is credited with saying, "Given one hour to save the world, I would spend fifty-five minutes defining the problem and five minutes finding the solution." While it is not my intention to devote

92 percent of the pages in this book to defining the problem, I think it is tremendously important to survey the foundations of society as we have started to do. It is only then that we will be able to have the predictive insights that will help us point our skates toward where the puck is going to be. Because today's problems are so complex, they can't be solved by being broken down into specific components. Instead, we should aim to move in the direction of the right next action given the information that we have.

How many industries that were around fifty years ago—and are still around today—are making their products in almost the exact same way? Can you think of an industry that uses almost the identical methods of production they did fifty years ago, one that hasn't undergone radical industrialization, innovation, or significant transformation? Very few. Why should financial services be excluded from this phenomenon? Whether we call this current era the Information Age or the Specialization Age, it's time to change the industry.

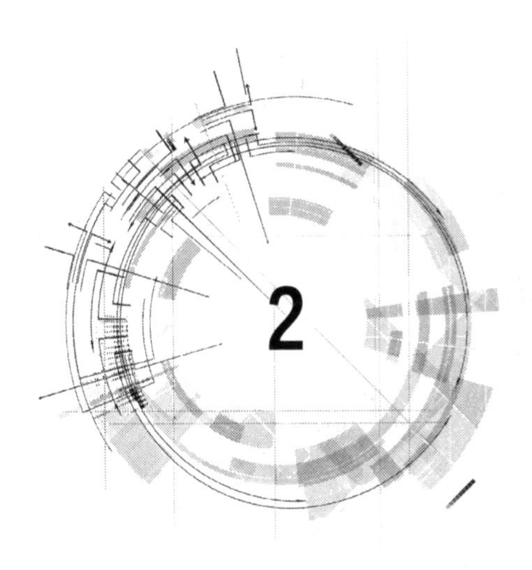

White Collars, Black Swans: The Failing Industry

In the twenty-first century, technology has triggered a reinvention of everything, from how we get our news to how we get our groceries. Industry after industry has been disrupted by new technology—education, media, telecom, retail, health care, and more have evolved as a result of its tremendous transformative influence.

Amazon disrupted bookstores and shopping malls. Uber dissed taxis, while Airbnb scorned hotels. News became "free," causing the fall of many media outlets, and self-publishing a la new print-on-demand tech triggered unexpected changes in the book industry.

Some traditional publishing houses closed, and others started self-publishing vanity presses to capture new markets. For the financial services industry, change came in the form of online stock trading sites and robo-advisors.

But I do not believe the financial services industry has been disrupted yet as it needs to be. Where a problem exists, there is always room for a solution, and I believe the industry is marked by a clear challenge that is begging for an answer. We are in a race to see who will discover the solution. Whether the hero will come in the form of the behemoth financial services corporations that ruled the latter half of the twentieth century or a financial services neophyte—one of the undiscovered Facebooks or Googles of the financial world—I do not know yet. What I do see is where the industry is failing consumers and where an opportunity for disruption exists.

The financial services industry is built on a promise—the promise that its practitioners will always do what's best for consumers. Yet the current nature of the industry makes this impossible.

THE UNKEPT PROMISE

The financial services industry doesn't provide guidance in the way that it claims to. In fact, there is a terrible, industrywide fixation on leading people to believe it's doing something that it's not.

It all begins with how we in financial services position ourselves to the overall public. We lead with a title that implies we are there to give our clients impartial advice; we call ourselves *financial advisors*, *financial consultants*, or *money managers*. In fact, we are more often glorified salespeople guiding consumers toward a particular product—life insurance, mutual funds, lines of credit, or annuities, to name a few—the sale of which benefits us as much as (if not more than) the customer.

My favorite is the mortgage broker who is selling loans yet calls himself an advisor. What if you were searching for a wardrobe consultant and someone said to you, "I'm a clothing advisor but I specialize in socks. I have many different kinds of socks, but that's all I've got." You probably wouldn't hire the sock expert! And yet consumers find themselves in essentially these situations, unknowingly hiring "financial advisors" all the time without realizing their limitations.

These limitations include the following:

- The advisor is selling a single product or set of products when consumers need the whole array.
- The advisor is incentivized by a sales commission rather than being rewarded for time and counsel.
- The advisor lets a product be the focal point of the relationship, therefore driving the conversation into uncomfortable, sales-based exchanges.
- The advisor is so salesy that the consumer is put off and builds up an aversion to anyone claiming to offer financial advice.

Fixing any one of these things will not bring about the solution to the problem of a mismatch between the need for true financial advice and the ability of the self-proclaimed financial expert to meet that need; it's a complex issue we face. What I'm calling for is a comprehensive overhaul of the financial services industry.

Multiple problems need to be brought into focus and solved. The last one on the list denoted above—putting off consumers with a salesy approach—is particularly important. It has led a good portion of the population to shut themselves off from valuable financial knowledge that could help them. This disengagement has resulted in many people being financially illiterate and yet trying to put their financial houses in order all on their own. This phenomenon can lead people to procrastinate in managing their money, too, which can be quite harmful.

Time is the best friend of an investor. Time allows interest to compound on deposits, it allows the values of stocks and bonds and precious metals to increase, and it offers time for a correction should a specific investment not perform as it should. Because of this, procrastination isn't just a bad idea: it's a thief, stealing both money and opportunity.

I think that if most financial advisors could, they would provide better, broader services. It's just that customizing financial advice for an individual customer's situation takes quite a bit more work than the time they are allotted allows, and such personalization is a deviation from industry norms. Einstein once said that your experience on this planet is defined by whether you believe this is a friendly universe or an unfriendly universe. I believe this is a friendly universe. I believe that most advisors mean well. That said, some issues, such as tax structures, advanced estate planning, and even some savings strategies are so complicated that those who believe they are helping are actually hurting. You can have the best intentions and still wind up with a bad outcome based on ignorance.

How did we get here?

THE RISE AND FALL OF THE CORPORATION

Not long ago, most people who wanted to get ahead in life believed they could do so by securing employment with the government or a corporation. People were rewarded and promoted solely on the basis of their mastery of processes and rules. Everybody and everything became organizationally dependent. This focus on large groups formally working together in precise ways to achieve a common goal reached its apex during the years immediately after World War II. After all, the military is literally a regimented organization and hierarchical in nature. Moreover, in many ways, the allied war effort showed what such groups at their most productive and powerful could accomplish. Everybody was mobilized around a single goal, and they knew that the collective power of large organizations was necessary to secure the victory.

When young soldiers came back from the war, they raced to secure stable white-collar jobs in massive corporations. These jobs represented the ticket to middle-class prosperity—a way to support a suburban lifestyle for their young families. The result was that large organizations acquired unprecedented social and cultural influence; the dominant cultural image of this age was thousands of men dressed in the same gray suit getting off a train and walking to their desk jobs at corporate offices.

The result was that large organizations acquired unprecedented social and cultural influence.

While citizens were going to work at corporations, they were also turning to corporations to manage their money. The likes of JP Morgan & Co., Bear Stearns, and Merrill Lynch found their calling by connecting Wall Street to Main Street and guiding the increased demand for capital management.

Over the twentieth century, the financial services industry and its institutions thus became a mainstream part of everyday life for many people. Among other things, it helped encourage the rapid growth of an investor class in developed countries. This was certainly an achievement. Wealth management enabled capital to reach around the world. It didn't matter what these groups of people had in common. Nothing was needed other than a desire to make money. This led to an ever-increasing ability to enact change with money, whether for good or for bad.

However, the baby boomer generation increasingly began to resist the "organization man" lifestyle. They wanted more opportunities to assert their individualism, the most extreme examples of this trend being the hippies and student radicals. With time, this celebration of the individual gradually became widespread, challenging the older culture of conformity. Then something happened that nobody could have predicted. The advent of the tech industry in the 1970s revolutionized the social and economic landscape, weakening large organizations and further elevating the individual.

A TARNISHED REPUTATION: THE PONZI OF ALL PONZI SCHEMES

Money management has gotten a bad rap. First of all, it's perceived to be expensive. Second, financial advice has been contaminated by fine print, hidden charges, and undisclosed conflicts of interest. And third, aren't all investment-type people fast-talking, morally questionable people, anyway? Old stereotypes don't die easily, especially when they are periodically reinforced by highly public stories of unscrupulous advisors taking advantage of their trusting clients. Cue Bernie Madoff.

Bernie Madoff propagated the most significant known white-collar financial fraud in history. The mastermind behind the plan, Madoff set up a classic Ponzi scheme that betrayed more than four thousand account holders. Perhaps most heartbreakingly, not only did Madoff lose the life savings of Holocaust survivor Elie Weisel, he also lost $15.2

million from Weisel's charitable organization, the Elie Weisel Foundation for Humanity.[1] A Ponzi or pyramid scheme is a fraudulent investment operation in which the operator generates returns for earlier investors through revenue paid by new investors rather than from legitimate business activities or profits made by financial trading. Operators of Ponzi schemes can be either individuals or corporations, and they grab the attention of new investors by offering short-term returns that are either abnormally high or unusually consistent. Between the promised returns and the positive word of mouth from people who truly believe they are benefiting from the scheme, the operator ensures that, until the scheme grows too large to be sustainable, there is no shortage of new investors.

Although Madoff's Ponzi scheme had been under suspicion and almost discovered several times in the decades he had run it, it was not until the financial crisis of 2008 that Madoff could no longer fund his clients' redemptions and the pyramid began to crumble. Arrested on December 11, 2008, Madoff pled guilty to eleven federal crimes. On further investigation, prosecutors estimated he had defrauded investors of $65.8 billion. Supplementary criminal charges included securities fraud, investment advisor fraud, mail fraud, wire fraud, money laundering, false statements, perjury, making fraudulent filings with the Securities and Exchange Commission (the regulatory body that is supposed to protect investors from fraudulent or manipulative practices and promote full disclosure), and theft from an employee benefit plan. He was sentenced to 150 years in a prison and ordered to forfeit over $170 billion in assets.

Madoff's story explains why large chunks of the population have chosen to stay away from financial professionals. I don't blame them. Madoff is the financial services equivalent of the boogeyman, only Madoff is real. I left a position at a large wirehouse because I hated having to answer twenty minutes' worth of headline-related questions before I could get to anything that would add value for the client. Even at my boutique financial services firm today, I sometimes have to explain to clients why they can feel safe entrusting us with their money, because of the backdrop of Madoff's massive fraud. If he could do it, they wonder, can't other financial professionals do the same?

Two recurring themes in investing are transparency and avoiding conflicts of interest. A fairly simple way to ensure both is to make sure assets are held in custody by a third party. Many financial services companies offer custody services as part of a bundled service platform under one agreement; Madoff did. He assumed both investment management and custodial responsibilities, which allowed him to forge statements. By using a third-party custodian, you are entering a safekeeping arrangement by bringing in another party. My current firm does this with Wells Fargo Clearing Services. In addition to the natural challenges the financial services industry faces as it evolves, it must also overcome challenges created by those like Madoff—and the other nefarious players in the 2008 financial crisis—who have broken consumer trust.

A GROWING DISTANCE BETWEEN SUPPLY AND DEMAND

Fast forward to the Specialization Age. Over time, as the tech industry revolutionized things like how people shop, communicate with each other, and send money, new business competitors entered the marketplace. These new and competitive entities catered more and more to the individual's needs, and the individual got used to speed and customization. Suddenly, the traditional corporate entities of the past didn't hold nearly as much appeal as the entrepreneurial start-ups that emerged with tech built into their offerings from the start.

The financial industry has been one of the slowest to adapt to the changes precipitated by tech. This is a real problem for the industry, because consumers don't just compare experiences from bank to bank, insurance provider to insurance provider, or brokerage firm to brokerage firm. They compare all of the experiences they have to one another. "If Amazon can ship me my purchase in two days," consumers wonder, "Why does it take five to seven business days for my bank to send me a new debit card?" "Why do I have to pay a $4 fee to withdraw cash from the ATM when I can use Venmo to pay a friend without a transaction fee?" As tech has innovated certain industries, the consumer starts to expect the same benefits from other industries. The prize of new business now goes to whichever company learns to most efficiently fold in tech and best meet consumer demands.

I believe that supply and demand in the financial services industry are now the furthest apart they have ever been. What people are demanding is so far from what is being offered, they end up having to settle if they want to get any help in putting their financial house in order. There hasn't been enough evolution with the supply to give consumers all these things they demand. But consumers in the financial services industry won't have to settle forever. Disruptors will appear, and if the financial services industry keeps allowing Silicon Valley to shepherd their innovation, banks will eventually lose. Someone other than the banks will come in and provide the total solution for consumers, and that innovator could end up being Apple, Google, Amazon, or someone else.

A RELUCTANT FINANCIAL SERVICES INDUSTRY

Why has the financial services industry been slow to adapt to the Specialization Age? A lot of it has to do with government regulation, but it also has to do with people already established in the industry getting really anxious when their pasts have become bigger than their futures. These executives don't want to give up their current ways of life and work.

Much has been written about the aversion to change in corporate settings, so I won't go further here. All you need to know is that decision-makers in today's marketplace have a vested interest in keeping things the same. Unfortunately for them, much like what has happened in the Rust Belt states, where technology and automation replaced factory workers, many folks in the financial services industry will be out of a job when the market catches up to them. Like trying to install new appliances in a home with a very old electrical system, remaining with old financial methods and models limits the ultimate results. It is only a matter of time until consumers demand more.

The big question is, Can these people evolve? I believe that a fraction of the people working in the financial marketplace today have the ability to evolve, but the rest lack the willingness or competence to do so. It is vitally important to point out that this is my opinion based on my experience. I'd estimate that one out of every ten people I meet in this industry appears to have the willingness and competence to change, but the other nine don't.

Increasingly, people are becoming aware that being connected to administrative structures—think large corporations and government—limits their ability to control their lives. Large organizations, by their very nature, lead to a loss of optimism, creativity, usefulness, and value wherever they influence people's lives; in a recent study of the "blight of bureaucracy," getting a new initiative off the ground in a company of a thousand or more employees was reported to be "not easy" or "very difficult" by 96 percent of respondents.[2] Escaping from governmental dependency means adopting entrepreneurial attitudes and developing entrepreneurial capabilities. The financial advisors of the future—what I call the *financial experience advisors*—will increasingly become the "freedom coaches" who enable millions of individuals to plan, make decisions, and take actions that lead to more liberated living based on entrepreneurial principles. However, financial advisors will only be able to do this if they have already liberated their own work and lives from corporate and governmental control. They can no longer be salespeople pushing the agenda of the Big Boss Corporation. They need to meet the needs of the consumer, the individual.

The financial advisors of the future will increasingly become the "freedom coaches" who enable millions of individuals to plan, make decisions, and take actions that lead to more liberated living based on entrepreneurial principles.

In their disconnected state, traditional financial advisors may, in a well-intentioned attempt to meet the demands of today, offer a longer menu of products and services than they have in the past. However, they do so without providing customized counsel, as if simply offering more choices is necessarily better. More choices without useful counsel only exacerbates consumer's challenge today of information overwhelm. If someone is trying to find a needle in a haystack, adding more hay to the stack only makes the problem worse. Consumers need not just choice, but expert support assessing the many options.

In contrast, for the financial experience advisor, each product and service has to be put in the context of the client's overall financial plan. The prime focus is the interplay of products and services as they are used to address a client's complete financial equation over the course of a long and mutually beneficial relationship.

What has been lost in much of modern financial services is a customer-centric service. Many financial advisors will never be able to evolve to the point of offering such individualized service and you, as a consumer, need to be aware of this so you know that if the fit doesn't feel right, you need to keep looking.

THE IMPLICATION: LEADERS DO NOT UNDERSTAND CUSTOMER SERVICE

Most of the leaders of the financial corporations that dominated the twentieth century were educated and trained to climb to the top. Their business school educations focused on systems, not people. Business success was described as a mastery of systems, not a mastery of human relationships. The same education that gets business leaders to the top focuses on quantity, not quality: What cannot be measured and counted does not matter. In corporate environments, individuals who know the numbers are admired and given control of the activities and futures of those who do not. Achieving a mastery of systems and figures leaves many with the attitude that relationships are merely tools for advancement. Being friendly is a strategy for promotion rather than a commitment to true friendship.

Once an individual sets out on the road to advancement up the corporate ladder, it is a lifelong commitment. Everything that happens inside of the business structure takes on political importance. A wrong move, at any time, can have serious consequences. Saying no is usually more advantageous than saying yes, because if you don't try, you can't fail. Bringing someone else down is a good way to build oneself up. What happens outside of the company is always of lesser daily importance than what is going on inside of it. Twenty years in the corporate grind is the usual time span for someone to reach a position of critical leadership. Big payoffs await those with the aptitude and the right attitudes. However, this apprenticeship takes its toll.

As time goes on, the financial services person working within the corporation becomes more and more disconnected from the noncorporate world, the place where most human beings experience and live their lives. The real world of dangers, opportunities, and strengths—of open-ended conversations, possibilities, and futures—becomes a foreign land for those climbing the corporate ladder. The real danger for these corporate folks lies in their disconnection from the experience of the average person, which renders them unable to perceive what consumers really need today.

As time goes on, the financial services person working within the corporation becomes more and more disconnected from the noncorporate world, the place where most human beings experience and live their lives.

It is not that corporate executives do not have real experiences and aspirations. It is just that they have had to focus for so long on such a narrow pursuit of such a rare prize in such an unnatural interpersonal environment that they have lost the ability to communicate and relate in many typical ways. What life is like outside the artificial reality of the corporation is hard for them to grasp and respond to. They are not bad people; they are just increasingly disconnected from the lives and issues of the clients and customers who purchase their products.

As the tech revolution speeds up, the disconnection between corporate executives and consumers will widen. Consumers will continue to demand services and experiences, such as on-demand support and personalized smartphone apps, that the leaders of the corporations, set in their ways as they are, will continue to drag their feet to avoid providing. This level of disconnection creates fertile ground for transformation, and the direction of this evolution for the financial services industry is already beginning to show itself in its new products, new services, and new models. As time goes on, competitors and disruptors will continue to challenge the status quo. People like you will continue to become better educated and, in turn, have higher expectations for the value they receive from their advisors. That's why you're reading this book, right?

AN INDUSTRY OF SILOS

One of the issues that has made it difficult for financial services to be customer-centric is that the industry operates in a set of distinct silos—investments, insurance, banking products, retirement, tax help, legal assistance, and so on (see Figure 2.1). It is virtually impossible to meet all of a customer's financial needs in a single silo, because each silo provides only one type of financial service.

The silo effect actually goes back pretty far; Adam Smith wrote about it in *Wealth of Nations* when he discussed the division of labor. The idea is that entities that operate within their core competencies will do better than those that try to do everything.

As the modern financial services industry emerged, different entities naturally specialized. Government regulation ensured certain services stayed in separate silos. For example, you had your friendly neighborhood insurance salesman, the local banker provided you with a home loan, and your broker put in your buy and sell orders.

It is easier to regulate silos, because each silo's specialized activity can be matched up with its corresponding specialized regulating agency or agencies. Silos maintain some level of organization across bureaucratic lines. When I worked at Deutsche Bank, when you were on the investment side of the house, there was a literal wall between the banking and commercial sides, and your badge would work on only one of them. This division represents the remains of the Glass-Steagall Act, which separated commercial and investment banking. The regulators wanted that wall to be there. The silo, in effect, is often both figurative and literal.

Figure 2.1: Industry Silos

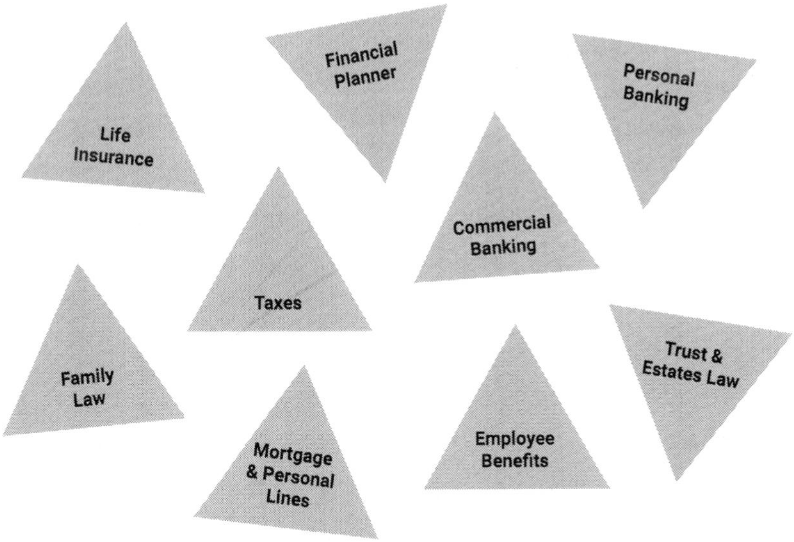

The result is a pseudo-spiderweb of advisors who help consumers navigate problems by reacting to life's challenges as they come.

Why this regulation-created siloing? The system of financial regulation is complex and fragmented. Responsibility to regulate the financial services industry is split between about a dozen federal agencies, hundreds of state agencies, and numerous industry-sponsored self-governing associations. This division started at the very beginning of the United States: during the Constitutional Convention, the founding fathers fragmented authority over financial markets between federal and state governments. That legacy survives today, complicating efforts to create a financial system that could function effectively. Regulatory jurisdictions often overlap, so most financial firms report to multiple regulators, yet gaps still exist in the supervisory structure, such that some firms report to few or, at times, no regulator. The overlapping jumble of standards; laws; and federal, state, and private jurisdictions can confuse even the most sophisticated student of the system. The result is a pseudo-spiderweb of advisors who help consumers navigate problems by reacting to life's challenges as they come.

From a high-level view, it seems that tradition or "we have always done it this way" plays a major role in the formation and perpetuation of silos. In my experience, one of the major factors keeping silos in place is trust—or, rather a lack of it. It is hard for anyone or any organization to give up control over a task that they are used to being responsible for.

The benefits from specialization are real, of course, and few people could make a good case against specialization. The financial solutions needed today, however, are so complex that specialists must work together for everyone's efforts to truly support the client.

The reality is this: Most adults have collected a series of products—some life insurance with one company, an IRA at another, a college account at a third institution, and so on—a basket of stuff that was acquired piecemeal as needs or opportunities arose. The products filling their basket are neither coordinated, nor organized, nor thoroughly evaluated for their ability to help these people reach their financial goals. Someone said, "You need this," and after some paperwork, into the basket it went. Maybe they slept better for a while knowing it was there. Frankly, they really don't know the purpose or function of half the instruments they've acquired. The phoenix of financial freedom is not going to arise from such a mess without some outside help.

To get the most out of their money and to reach their life goals, these basket-hauling consumers need a silo-savvy professional to sift through what they have acquired and help them evaluate what they have and figure out what they still need. This is where the financial experience advisor comes in.

THE DEATH OF THE SALES, MAN

No one wants to be sold to any more. This is due to the sales process of past decades being sullied by poor practitioners of the craft. These were salespeople determined to make the sale regardless of the needs of the customer. Alas, some folks like these are still around today. We've all run into pushy salespeople who are clearly more interested in their commission than they are in helping us. People like these lose our trust.

I've run into these types throughout my career. Looking back, I can recall many financial advisors who did not want to spend too much up-front time with a prospective client. They did not really care any more about the client's situation than what was needed to make a product presentation and, ultimately, a sale. They made a good living, but their superficiality always bothered me. Over the last decade, I have noticed this same ethical ambivalence in many highly successful advisors who depend entirely on product sales for their income. They would say they wanted to treat each of their clients as unique individuals, but when it came down to actually serving them as unique individuals, it was obvious that their clients just represented a commission. Their concern would then shift to the next client and sale, with no looking back.

Because advisors are paid only for selling commodities, they have to treat their clientele like commodities.

As long as advisors only (or mostly) get paid for selling products—and only after the sale is official—they cannot give their clients the attention each one deserves. They cannot continually cultivate and deepen relationships over an extended period. The time is not available, because the method of compensation simply doesn't allow it. They are encouraged by the industry to make the relationships superficial and short, regardless of how much they might like it to be otherwise. Basing a compensation system on products sold rewards quantity, not quality. Because advisors are paid only for selling commodities, they have to treat their clientele like commodities. In the process, advisors feel superficial, cheap, and unprofessional; they feel that they, too, are just commodities—it's a terrible, vicious cycle.

So you see, it is in the very nature of businesses—from the inception of industrialization to the present day—to treat individuals in the marketplace like they are naive economic children. The financial industrial machine works best for big business when customers believe that their financial advisors, like fathers, know best. Corporations are cast as the powers that be, providing good things to the masses below.

A vast majority of executives, managers, and financial corporations are still operating in this tired organizational structure of the Industrial Age, even within an Information Age consumer environment. With each passing quarter, corporate management drifts further out of touch with the emerging issues of their financial clients and customers. Corporate executives at head offices seem incapable of having in-depth, back-and-forth conversations that would allow them to learn what clients truly want from their firms, so these executives have no idea that they need to set a new course so that their businesses can provide the financial products and services that are needed, not just the ones the firm has always offered.

This out-of-touch disposition denotes a fundamental breakdown in their relationship with the buying public. Since the executives and managers are becoming increasingly ignorant of what clients want, they enlist growing ranks of lawyers to protect them from making serious errors of judgment and execution that could damage their organization's reputation and viability, as well as their careers.

One of the major misconceptions prevalent today is that people are turning to financial advisors in growing numbers simply because more people are calling themselves advisors. Although that may be partially true, people actually started turning to financial advisors because of the growing complexity of their financial lives. The public has begun to realize that the people who have been selling them products for the past few decades actually haven't done much in the way of planning for them and that they need real assistance.

Although faced with a somewhat dismal economic outlook, especially those who still have 2008 on their minds, folks still want to accomplish all of their life goals. Consumers like you have made the conscious decision to not let the fear of striking out keep you from playing the game. While it is learning to focus more on goal achievement, the industry hasn't caught up. It fails to match multiple client goals to multiple investment strategies. Clients are forced to attempt to calculate what percentages of an overall portfolio they should allocate to specific individual goals. Market performance over the last decade has taught that they can't rely on the market to always move up. Investors today are focusing more on achieving their goals than on fretting about how the market performed. The thing is, if investors had the help of a financial services professional well-versed with the products of multiple silos who could look at their individual situations, take their financial goals to heart, and apply hard-won financial expertise to create a personalized financial plan, achieving their dreams would be easier (see Figure 2.2).

Figure 2.2: Multiple Silos Working Together

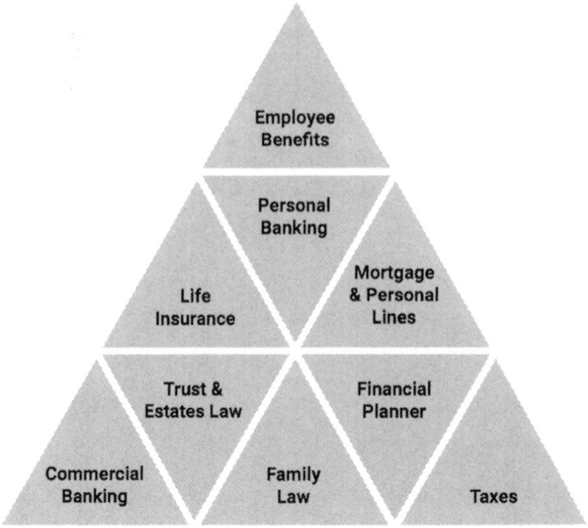

I dedicate the remainder of this book to helping financial services consumers make the shift into the Specialization Age. It will help consumers choose the right kind of financial services professional as well as educate themselves on key ways to manage one's financial experience in the Specialization Age. Professionals in the financial services industry can gain insight as well; I also explore the myriad ways the industry is being called to meet changing consumer demand.

NEXT-GENERATION SOLUTIONS FOR THE INDUSTRY

- **Eliminate conflicts of interest.** If your advisor packages him- or herself as always doing what's in the best interest of the client, make sure that conflicts of interest have truly been removed from the equation. I'm not only talking about kickbacks and incentives. I believe this issue of what's best for the client should be tackled head-on, at the foundation, by adjusting one key factor: how advisors get paid. For example, if your advisor is paid by taking a percentage of assets under management and you ask your advisor if you should take money out of your investments to pay off your mortgage, in the current structure, he or she is incentivized to say no because that advisor will take a pay cut if you do. Alternatively, if you ask whether you should sell your investment property and move the proceeds to your investments, you will be advised to do so because the result will be that your advisor will get a pay raise. Here is a solution: Only hire advisors who are willing to be paid on the basis of your net worth. They then will be incentivized to make sure you make really good decisions with your investments, mortgage, 401(k), and other financial products. Billing based on net worth forces accountability, eliminates conflicts of interest, and allows the advisor to execute on holistic financial planning. We'll be better off if the term *commission* disappears. That being said, it may take some time for compensation via net worth to catch on. An interim option as the industry evolves, which could also work more long-term for those with a smaller net worth, is to work with advisors who simply charge fees for their time.

- **Replace the antiquated sales process.** Advisors should consider offering education and value for free with no strings attached, like the rest of the marketplace does, in order to build trust. Note that I'm not talking about the classic "lunch and learn": I'm referring to free seminar content, YouTube videos, and webinars. In these sessions and videos, there should be, at most, a one-sentence call to action: enough with half the presentation being focused on sales. Advisors need to make the paradigm shift so that the first thought through the mind of a consumer invited to watch one of these presentations is not "oh boy, I'm going to be sold to," but rather "I need to click so I can learn more." I wholeheartedly believe that advisors should be providing general knowledge for people for free—not giving away any sort of proprietary information or intellectual property, just education. All of this knowledge is already free, if you can find it (thank you, Google!). It's time to get away from the old-guard attitude. The first step is creating content that shows—and shares—what we know.

- **Move from a consumer-based or commission-based society to an experience-based society—that is what the Specialization Age is all about.** In traditional financial advisory firms, the culture has been sales-based and cut-throat, holding each employee to making certain sales quotas and creating an internal competition among advisors to get the highest numbers. The faster an advisor cycles through clients and the more products one sells, the more reward the advisor is given. In the process, the client experience is lost and his or her financial needs are glossed over, maybe even ignored. In the next generation of advisory services, I see the majority of advisors as being paid a salary to manage a certain group of clients to whom they would be reaching out on a regular basis that works for the client (e.g., quarterly, semi-annually). The firm would structure the agreements between clients and advisors, administer payment and paperwork, and provide the overall structure needed to facilitate this relationship. Meetings between advisor and client would be a top priority so that the two are collaborating to build the client's 3D financial plans for his or her desired financial household. In this setting, the client experience is honored, and his or her financial needs are truly considered. The internal organizational culture at the advisory firm becomes more collegial too, with a culture of commission replaced by a culture of collaboration. It's a subtle but major shift that trickles down into client relationships and allows for the space that is needed to create meaningful experiences.

THE WAY THINGS WERE (AND WEREN'T)

When this book was written, the childhood years of most people in decision-making roles fell somewhere between 1950 and 1975. During this period, one could graduate from high school and go to work in plants or mills. Moreover, these were great jobs! By your midtwenties, you had earned enough to buy a home and start a family. You could work for forty-five years and be taken care of by the corporation, the union, or the government. All your financial planning was done for you. If you needed a loan for your house or your children's education, the corporation provided it, along with your health insurance and a retirement pension. Generous union contracts made these benefits possible.

Many people think this situation lasted for a long time. However, the financial promise was only completely fulfilled during a twenty-five-year period after the Second World War, when American corporations in all industries were at the top of the world markets. Rich labor contracts were possible because so much money was being made.

Organizations, feeling confident, promised lifetime employment and benefits to millions of workers.

By the mid-1970s, the industrial economic model that supported this idyllic arrangement began to weaken; today, it has largely disintegrated. At the beginning of the boom, most of America's economic competition had been flattened or set back by World War II. By the 1970s, these competitors had re-entered the global marketplace, many of them with better, lower-priced products; more innovative production processes; and hungrier, lower-cost workforces. Tech-based tools and systems replaced many manual-labor and routine office jobs with much more efficient machinery in all parts of the industrial economy, from production lines to administrative departments.

As a result, consumers today don't have that graduation-to-grave assistance employers briefly provided.

In the wake of the extraordinary costs of the Vietnam War, President Nixon tried to protect the US dollar by disconnecting it from the gold standard. This action introduced a period of currency exchange turmoil throughout the world economy that caught financial officers of large corporations by surprise. The oil shocks of the mid-1970s drove up the costs of energy throughout the industrialized economy, introducing a period of severe inflation that hobbled many large corporations and even destroyed some that were burdened with debts and unfunded liabilities.

As a result, consumers today don't have that graduation-to-grave assistance employers briefly provided. Rather, they need a financial experience advisor who is going to help them with the fundamentals of their financial lives and then bring in other experts who will help check the boxes on all of the other important aspects of financial management. This means that financial experience advisors need to be able to connect their clients with accountants, an estate planning lawyer, a property and casualty person, insurance folks, and the like. Sooner or later, the consumer masses are going to demand this. Demand always precedes supply. If people demand this kind of holistic life planning of their advisor, they will quickly discover whether the advisor is helping them meet their goals or just selling them products.

There has been a lot of talk about holistic life planning for quite some time now, ever since the dot-com bubble burst. Yet people in the industry have overleveraged this concept, saying they are holistic advisors when they are not—they are product specialists. The bottom line is that a holistic advisor needs to create holistic plans. Anyone in the industry can actually do this: they simply need the ability to help people make smart decisions, a Rolodex full of the names of financial silo specialists they trust, and the determination to break out of their product specialist mold! They also need to be able to find strategic partners who will do a good job of delivering the right products that their clients need. This could be done at a large wirehouse or a boutique financial planning firm, and the financial experiences advisor, detailed in the next chapter, is the professional to do it.

CONCLUSION: LOOKING BENEATH THE SURFACE

Someone in my family used to say, "There's a difference between fishing and standing on the shoreline like an imbecile." That is, you can stand on the shore and throw a line in the water with no hook and people looking on may be fooled into thinking you're fishing when you're really not. Or, if you have bait on a hook specially selected for what you're fishing for, a prime spot on the shoreline, and you are able to cast properly, you could actually be fishing.

In the financial industry, there are a lot of people standing in the water with a line—how do you really know whether they are fishing? You have to ask them the right questions. When you do, you will find out that some of them have no bait on the hook, and others have a very distinct plan for what they are doing. When you ask the right questions (like those highlighted in Chapter 4), you will be able to figure out pretty quickly who's standing on the shoreline looking like an imbecile versus who's actually fishing.

I started this chapter talking about how traditional financial advisors are not living up to their promises. What they are doing is fishing with no bait. In the future, you're going to need someone with the smarts to know, metaphorically speaking, where the fish are and how to get them to bite. What you're going to need is a financial experience advisor.

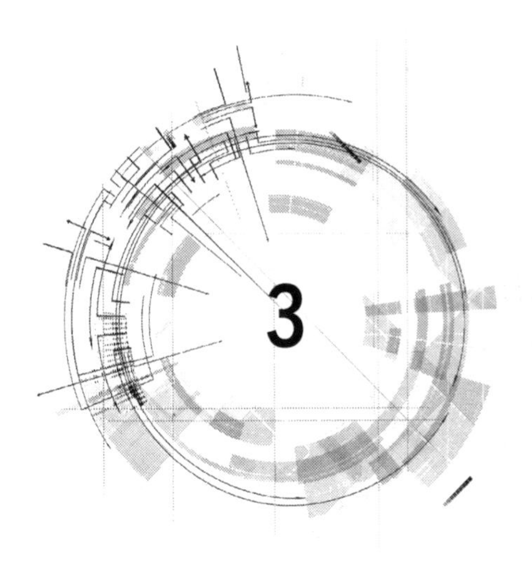

Atlas Arises: Financial Experience Advisors

The financial experience advisor is poised to disrupt the financial services industry. Unlike a traditional financial advisor, the financial experience advisor puts the client rather than the investment product first. Unlike the traditional financial advisor who works within one specialty, the financial experience advisor quarterbacks the whole financial team. Unlike the traditional financial advisor who sells to the client, the financial experience advisor provides real value, up front.

Think about it. In the Specialization Age, consumers are used to receiving free and useful advice on a daily basis from the many entities out there that are marketing to them: "Free webinars!" "Downloadable checklists!" "YouTube tutorials!" Do you think these very same consumers will gravitate toward the advisor who is using the old-school model of selling to the consumer or the financial experience advisor who understands that he or she must provide real value to the consumer to stay relevant? As soon as the marketplace delivers to the consumer the option of the financial experience advisor, disruption to traditional advising will follow.

As soon as the marketplace delivers to the consumer the option of the financial experience advisor, disruption to traditional advising will follow.

That's right, the financial experience advisor does not yet exist in mainstream fashion, at least not by title. Although the concept of the financial experience advisor started in my mind, aspects of the profession can already be found along a spectrum in the marketplace, with what I call the traditional financial advisor on one end and the financial experience advisor on the other end.

You can definitely find firms today that have people whose jobs include characteristics of the financial experience advisor; my firm, Centric Capital Advisors, where I serve as a partner, offers services that are probably the closest approximation of the financial experience advisor experience that's available right now. Is an army of perfect financial experience advisors marching out there in the world? Not yet, as that's not how the world works when a new trend is emerging. However, plenty of people who have the potential to be top-notch financial experience advisors are out there, unaware of this new job that would play well to their strengths but potentially ready to respond to the call for this new type of advisor.

Further, consumers know that they want financial experience advisors, if only subconsciously. They can perceive a gap in the services available from the financial industry, but they don't know what fits there. Luckily for them, this book fills in the gaps.

Demand exists for people to deliver the services of the financial experience advisor; certain advisors, like me, understand these demands, are anticipating the future trends, and offer financial experience advisor–like experiences. If you are in the market for a financial experience advisor right now, a time when financial experience advisors are an aspirational profession rather than an existing one, find instead a financial advisor with financial experience advisor characteristics. Maybe, as a result of your work together, you can be the client who clarifies your financial advisor's vision and moves him or her to expand offered services or modify his or her approach or philosophy, bringing that person's practice that much closer to the true financial experience advisor experience.

The idea for the financial experience advisor has emerged not in a vacuum but within the context the Specialization Age. Its seeds are real, and I am merely aiming to gather us all together to pour water and nutrients on it. I am confident that the financial experience advisor concept can and will come fully into fruition in the coming decade. My purpose for outlining it in this book is so that we, as financial professionals and consumers, can more consciously shape its emergence.

I hope to provide a heads-up to my peers so they have a chance to influence the evolution of the financial services industry and avoid losing ground in the same way that people and organizations in other disrupted industries have in the past couple decades. I also aim to inform you, the consumer, about the potential benefits of work with a financial experience advisor so that you can be on the lookout for financial experience advisor characteristics in the existing advisors out there today and in services of the future as they pop up. Now and then, you need to demand more of what you desire and need, because demand is what ultimately drives business innovation.

To that end, I describe my current vision for the financial experience advisor in this chapter. I encourage consumers and financial professionals alike to get in on the discussion. Professionals: Write articles, run webinars, host roundtables, and put together focus groups with your current client base. Consumers: Share this book with your friends and neighbors and talk about this shift from the traditional financial advisor to the financial experience advisor. Start a discussion. Post feedback via my website, www.atlas-shift.com, and ask me questions directly at info@atlas-shift.com. Now let's discuss the financial experience advisor and how this new breed of advisor is going to change all our lives for the better.

TRADITIONAL FINANCIAL ADVISOR VERSUS FINANCIAL EXPERIENCE ADVISOR

The best way to communicate exactly what the future is, is by comparing it with what came before. In the case of financial advisors, the traditional financial advisor is what came before. As I have touched on already, a traditional financial advisor sells specific products, while a financial experience advisor promotes financial solutions. Further, although a traditional financial advisor may offer a variety of products, each product is principally investment oriented. For financial experience advisors, the client's long-range financial goals and needs, determined through careful consideration of an up-to-date client profile, lead to the formation of an overarching plan. On the basis of the plan, the advisor identifies the different products and services the client needs and advises the client to acquire those products and services on the basis of that need, rather than because the product or service is what the advisor specializes in selling or because that product has the best commission or sales incentive. In short, the product is subsidiary to the plan. This represents an entirely different way of going about—and thinking about—the client–advisor relationship. Table 3.1 provides more insight into the differences between the traditional financial advisor and the financial experience advisor.

Table 3.1: The Traditional Financial Advisor versus the Financial Experience Advisor

Characteristic	Traditional Financial Advisor	Financial Experience Advisor
Foundation	Impersonal, one size fits all	Personal advice
Collaboration	Walled-off silo	Team player
Focus	Their business as it relates to you	Your objectives, related to their business and collaborators
Licensure	Typically a combination of Series 6, 7, and 63	Typically a Series 7 or 63; always a Series 65 or 66
Designations	CLU®, ChFC®, various other product designations	CFP®, CFA®, various other planning designations
Prioritization	Product over process	Tailor-made solutions

Note. Series 6 = Investment Company Products/Variable Contracts Limited Representative; Series 7 = General Securities Representative; Series 63 = Uniform Securities Agent Exam; Series 65 = Uniform Investment Advisor Exam; Series 66 = NASAA Uniform Combined State Law Exam; CLU® = Chartered Life Underwriter; ChFC® = Chartered Financial Consultant; CFP® = CERTIFIED FINANCIAL PLANNER; CFA® = Chartered Financial Analyst™.

Although it could take a white paper or even an entire book to define all of these designations in detail, I will provide a brief attempt at defining them here in the effort to make financial services more transparent to you, the consumer, so you can make enlightened choices. That is what being an atlas is all about.

The *Series 6* designation allows professionals to sell variable products such as variable life insurance and variable annuities; it also allows someone to sell you mutual funds, but *not* individual securities. In short, it is a packaged-products license. It is a license that someone can use to sell products that are easily sold based on suitability but not best interest. The *Series 7* designation means that a professional can sell you stocks, bonds, and options—all types of security products except for commodities and futures.

The *Series 63* designation allows a professional to sell you any type of security as long as they are registered within your state. *Series 65* allows someone to act as an investment advisor but not to sell you any securities. In other words, they can charge a fee for their advice, but they can't receive any fees for securities-related transactions. This is where the *Series 66* designation comes in: it combines the best of the Series 63 and the Series 65. With this designation, a professional can give you financial advice *and* help you with securities and other investments. A professional must have this designation to be a Registered Investment Advisor (RIA). The value of working with an RIA (versus a brokerage firm) is manifold; benefits include more transparency, ability to provide independent advice, and an incentive structure and fiduciary standard to always put you, the client first.[1]

The value of working with an RIA is manifold; benefits include more transparency, ability to provide independent advice, and an incentive structure and fiduciary standard to always put you, the client first.

The *CFA®* is a rigorous credential—some argue the most rigorous credential of all—one that is wholly focused on advanced investment analysis and portfolio management skills but has no comprehensive planning requirement. The *CFP®* is a broader designation than the CFA® in that it covers not just investment management, but also tax planning, insurance, retirement, and estate planning—all things personal finance. The CFP® covers the breadth of financial services so a professional can help people plan. The CFP® training and testing takes professionals a mile wide and a foot deep, whereas the CFA® training and testing takes professionals a foot wide and a mile deep, mainly on the portfolio side of things. The CFA® and the CFP® are both extremely difficult to get, with a rigorous exam and education schedule.

The *ChFC®* is an alternative to the CFP®. It was developed for those who wanted similar training to the CFP® without the need to study so intensively. It is similar to the CFP®, except instead of there being a comprehensive final exam, there are exams after each course. Lastly, the CLU® is a designation that prepares someone to sell you insurance products. Now that you have a better understanding of the different designations, take another look at Table 3.1 You can start to see how traditional financial advisors vary from financial experience advisors.

Stepping away from designations and focusing on the other elements of Table 3.1, I see traditional financial advisors as impersonal, in their own walled-off silo (not working or caring to work with the rest of your much-needed professional team), strictly focused on their own business as it relates to you, and oriented toward products.

This is contrasted by the financial experience advisor, who is personable, a team player (communicating with fellow advisors for a client's benefit), and focused on your objectives—not only as they relate to his or her business, but also on how they may require additional advisors to be brought in. Finally, they prioritize tailor-made solutions. The comparison can be summed up in a word: personalization. A traditional financial advisor has nearly none, and a financial experience advisor has as much as possible. Because of this differing focus, you see differently oriented practices (my product vs. your solution), differences in flexibility (my silo vs. part of your team), different licenses (products vs. planning), and a different demeanor toward you (professional but impersonal vs. friendly and professional).

A good example of a firm doing work in this vein is the one I am a partner in, Centric Capital Advisors (shameless plug). There are other firms out there like us in that they have a CFP® on staff who works in an RIA capacity. Since I believe the CFP® is so useful of a credential and can be so helpful to you the client, let's dig deeper into the meaning of the CFP®. Kaplan Educational explains the CFP® quite simply in the following lay terms: as professionals who work "with clients to create holistic long-term plans in order to help them meet their financial goals."[2] Depending on stage of life, the CFP® can help clients manage student-loan debt, save for a house, set up college savings for children, adjust tax strategies for a higher income, acquire life insurance, and plan for retirement—that is, plan for and manage money across life's stages and phases.

Depending on stage of life, the CFP® can help clients manage student-loan debt, save for a house, set up college savings for children, adjust tax strategies for a higher income, acquire life insurance, and plan for retirement.

What you should also know is that this exclusive designation is only awarded to those who have passed a rigorous set of certification requirements by the Certified Financial Planner Board of Standards, Inc. involving in-depth exams in the areas of financial planning, taxes, insurance, estate planning, and retirement.[3] The benefits of working with a CFP® include knowing your advisor must uphold their certification through continuing education—something to consider with new financial instruments appearing regularly on the consumer market, as well as abiding by the strict ethical requirement put forth by the board, along with knowing that they have the certification that is the most recognized in the industry for personal financial planning.

EXPERIENCES ARE SOUGHT IN THE AGE OF SPECIALIZATION

The Specialization Age is all about personalized experience—whether it's a personalized online shopping experience with everything you desire delivered to your door or a custom playlist booming through your speakers. Why are personalized experiences so important right now?

Tech makes everything it touches more complex, including every aspect of work and lifestyle. This impact increases the anxiety levels of the millions of people who are directly affected. To find relief from the stress stemming from increasing complexity, these individuals turn to a growing number of experiences that promise to be intellectually stimulating, psychologically rejuvenating, and emotionally satisfying. These can take the form of custom-designed and uniquely packaged vacations, shopping sprees, leisure therapies, hospitality adventures, or educational programs catering to multiple interests. The experience sector is the fastest growing segment of advanced economies.

Yet people are seeking experiences not just because of tech but because we live in a postindustrial society in which our lives are now saturated with things made in factories. I am reminded of Christmastime overload. I am sure I am not the only one among my peers who finds it a hassle to de-tag, store, organize, and maintain all those new things recently unwrapped under the tree. We are also generally more affluent as a Western society then we were in the past, and the Walmart effect has allowed many of us to enjoy having more stuff, with inexpensive goods at our disposal. Yet more things inevitably leads to clutter ("Where did I put that thing?!") and, you guessed it, stress ("I cannot believe the widget already broke!"). This being the Specialization Age, though, there are already businesses catering to organizing (think Marie Kondo's *The Life-Changing Magic of Tidying Up*), decluttering (*Clean House* spent ten seasons on the Style Network), and pulling back on the conspicuous consumption (the tiny house movement shows no signs of abating). This shows that even if your goal is to uncomplicate your life by owning less, there's a specialist to help you make your dream come true.

To make their products more desirable by differentiating them from the mass-produced, cheap goods that are starting to seem like more of a bane than a boon, some companies are catching on to the customers' desire for personalization. Options for having jeans custom-made already exist, through online retailers like itailor.com, customadejeans.com, and zipfitdenim.com. Nike offers the opportunity to choose different colors for different parts of your shoes, and you can even add your own initials.[4] Reebok lets you mix and match customized colors and materials.[5] Building to these specifications is certainly a start. But how about getting shoes sized exactly to each of your feet? With 80 percent of the population having one foot larger than their other,[6] it may only be a matter of time before people are able to order customized left- and right-shoe sizes.

Point being, people want the custom experience these days, but the financial industry is resistant to this approach because customization comes at a variable price, which means the bottom line for any transaction, not to mention the quarterly earnings, are much less predictable. When it comes to the financial services industry, an additional challenge emerges from the existence of silos—investments are separate from insurance that is separate from estate planning and so on. How can you offer clients a customized package of financial products when you don't sell all of them? It is time to do the creative thinking and the heavy lifting needed to break down the walls and have different financial service professionals working together on behalf of the consumer. It is time to offer custom-made solutions for consumers' complex financial lives. It is time for the financial experience advisor.

IT'S ALL ABOUT THE TEAM

Within the financial services industry, the challenge to providing a personalized experience to the client is all of our silos. In the United States, the various specialties—insurance, banking, investments, trusts—have, especially since the Great Depression, traditionally been kept separate from one another by legislation. It is only in the last two decades that competition has crossed the boundaries of these different sectors, thanks to deregulation and innovation. For most of the Industrial Revolution, many of the corporations in the financial services sector ran in a virtually competition-free environment. Internally, many of them were run like socialist utopias. Externally, they were managed like quasi-public utilities. This approach did not emphasize capability, achievement, and innovation. Financial services at the corporate level proved an excellent breeding ground for complacency, incompetence, and self-satisfied stasis. This stagnation curtailed adaptation to the times, leading to irrelevance.

The solution for our fragmented industry is having the advisor shift into a new role as the quarterback of a client's financial strategies. In particular, the key to success is that a financial experience advisor will have a network of highly specialized professionals who are able to meet a client's advanced planning needs—such as estate planning, wealth protection, and charitable giving—so that the financial experience advisor can focus on the client's investment management needs, secure in the knowledge that all facets of a client's financial picture are being addressed.

Here are the team members of the financial experience of the future (also see Figure 3.1):

1. *Financial experience advisor.* This is the general manager of the team of free-agent professionals. The goal of this team is straightforward: to help the client address his or her most pressing needs in the areas of advanced planning. As the general manager of the network, the financial experience advisor has three primary roles:

- To build the network and manage it on an ongoing basis
- To provide the network members with a deep understanding of the client
- To facilitate the meetings with network members to draw out the optimal recommendations and outcomes for clients

2. *The atlas.* This is the client, the person the financial team is coming together to help. The atlas, though, is not a helpless naïf. An atlas has a vision for his or her financial goals and future, and the atlas is smart enough to realize that to achieve one's objectives, it's a good idea to ask experts to put together a roadmap showing how to get there. The atlas communicates clearly and often with the team so everyone remains on the same page and strategies can be tweaked as goals or life situations change.

3. *A private client lawyer.* The private client lawyer will be a key member of the professional network. That's because this expert will address many of the most critical areas of concern for clients—including tax planning, estate planning, and legal needs.

Private client lawyers are not the trusts and estates lawyers employed by private banks or life insurance companies. Instead, more often than not, they are partners at high-end boutique firms. The typical high-end private client lawyer should be able to provide the following services:

- Estate planning
- Wealth protection planning
- Income tax planning
- Succession planning
- Business planning for successful entrepreneurs
- Charitable giving program development
- Administration services (tied to the above planning services)
- Probate services
- Guardianship and conservatorship services

4. *An accountant.* While the private client lawyer will provide a big-picture perspective on tax planning for things like estates and trusts, the accountant typically will have much more detailed, day-to-day

knowledge of a client's income taxes. He or she should be able to make specific recommendations to mitigate these taxes.

5. *A life insurance specialist.* A good life insurance specialist will work closely with the private client lawyer to identify areas of the client's financial life needing protection and then structure solutions that leverage the entire range of life insurance solutions. To avoid any potential for conflict, this specialist should not offer investments.

Beyond the five members of the network described above, a wide range of other professionals could also be called upon by a financial experience advisor. These can be a personal lines insurance specialist—a property-casualty agent who works at the very high end of the market—a mortgage lender, an actuary, a valuation specialist, real estate brokers, a collaborative divorce specialist team, and more.

Figure 3.1: The Financial Experience Advisor's Team

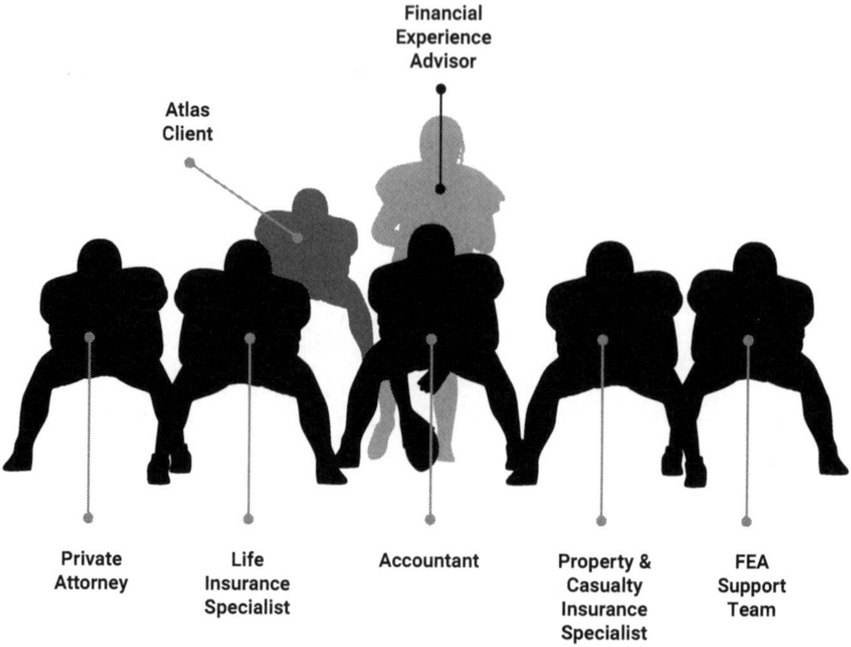

It is time for the professionals who are holding themselves out as wealth managers and financial advisors to become the metaphorical CFO for their client's families. They need to evolve, expand their skill sets, truly get to know their clients, and become the one that quarterbacks clients' financial goals.

THE ATLAS CLIENT: FINANCIAL SELF-EMPOWERMENT IN THE SPECIALIZATION AGE

At some point between the Roman Empire and now, people went from storing money under their mattresses to handing it over to banks. Banks kept money safe, and, more recently, the government insured the banks so people could count on their money being there when it was needed. People were further supported by the creation of government safety nets like Social Security in the 1930s and Medicare in the 1960s, so people could receive a small income and be cared for in old age.

The rise of the retirement pension by corporations and government organizations added another layer of security, as did the start of an investor class, a culture in which people set aside money, invested it in the markets, and watched it grow into a nest egg they could draw on in their retirement years. Brokerage houses advised people on when to buy and sell, and people received visits from their friendly neighborhood life insurance salesman reminding them to make sure their loved ones were covered after they left this mortal coil. In short, the government and the marketplace took steps to keep peoples' financial experiences on track.

Then came the Information Age and the emergence of a global marketplace. Markets became increasingly interconnected, and new financial instruments were born. Technology allowed faster transactions, and the consumer gained access to more information.

Access to information is good, but too much information can become an unusable deluge. Complex markets offer new opportunities, but consumers are understandably unsure about how to leverage them. Today, there is no more hiding one's life savings under the mattress, but there is also no more blindly giving all the money to the broker, either. A new kind of partnership is required between the financial advisor and the client.

Consumers need advisors to help them navigate the complex marketplace of financial services, but they also need to play a hands-on role in making sure their money is managed in a way that truly supports their desired financial experience. If not, they run the risk of advisors using outmoded methods that won't provide desired outcomes, such as retirement savings that don't last for tomorrow's longer life spans or investment portfolios that are not truly diversified given today's interconnected global marketplace. That's right: Atlas clients may hire advisors to provide assistance and advice on how to achieve their desired financial experiences, but they aren't handing off the entire responsibility of managing their money. Rather, they're lightening their financial load but ultimately responsible for ensuring their advisor is following the roadmap they've developed together and adjusting the route as life circumstances change.

Today, there is no more hiding one's life savings under the mattress, but there is also no more blindly giving all the money to the broker, either.

As we make the transition from the Information Age to the Specialization Age, consumers must demand more from their financial advisors and hold them accountable for the needs of today. Even when the financial services industry makes the shift and financial experience advisors become the norm, clients still have to remain engaged. We are in an age where each person's desired financial experience is unique; the only way to receive a customized experience is to be involved in its creation.

I call this new kind of engaged client an *atlas* for the following reasons. He or she has made what I call the *atlas shift* from the Information Age to the Specialization Age. As the map of the financial landscape has been redrawn, he or she has made the mental and economic shift from believing "there's a safety net" to believing "my success and well-being is dependent on me." Like Atlas, the Titan in Greek mythology who was responsible for holding up the sky, the atlas client understands that he or she must play a key role in ensuring one's own financial security now and in the years to come. In a future where Social Security has dwindled and pensions have been replaced by personal savings, this mental shift of responsibility is necessary.

Last, many of us want to have a positive impact on the world. To do so, we must begin by putting our own houses in order. If you want to enact any social or environmental change, you have to start with yourself. Unlike the mythical Atlas commanded to hold up the sky, today's atlas financial consumers choose to take responsibility for their financial experiences. They know that this involves effort, discipline, and hard work, but they are motivated by the reward—a custom-made financial experience that supports them and their desired life.

THE TIES THAT BIND

Within the personalized financial experience, we can still find commonalities around key issues. These commonalities can focus the financial experience advisor's work. I find that people tend to worry, to varying degrees, about the following financial issues (also see Figure 3.2):

1. Making smart decisions with their money on a day-to-day basis
2. Mitigating the impact of taxes
3. Ensuring that heirs, parents, children, and grandchildren are taken care of
4. Keeping wealth safe from potential creditors, litigants, children's spouses, and potential ex-spouses, as well as from catastrophic losses
5. Being able to give to a charitable cause

Unfortunately, 2–5 don't matter if you don't do 1. This is why financial experience advisors need to be the quarterback of an entire wealth management team.

Figure 3.2: The Financial Experience Pyramid

As the quarterback of the wealth management team, the financial experience advisor is responsible for helping you make smart decisions with your money day in and day out and then assembling the team of professionals, such as lawyers, accountants, life insurance specialists, and a business manager, who can help you achieve your remaining goals. There may have been a point in time when people could have figured out financial management themselves, but today the financial landscape is too complex to navigate without a guide.

Consumers need someone to listen to their goals, help them figure out what is most important to them, and facilitate meetings with the CPA, the attorney, and so on—a network of individuals, built by the financial experience advisor, who can help. The different professionals in the network can be interchangeable if a client has already worked with one, like a CPA, whom he or she already likes and trusts. But the financial experience advisor has a network that he or she extends to the client to make sure that the financial experience advisor delivers on the promise to serve the best interest of the client.

I am reminded of the family office, which has investment professionals, lawyers, and accountants under one roof, usually servicing extremely high-net-worth individuals. You may be wondering how the family office avoids the silo trap. The Family Office Rule, Rule 202(a)(11)(G)-l), excludes qualifying family offices from regulation under the Investment Advisers Act of 1940. The complexity of an average person's financial life has gotten to be so great that we all could use a family office! Yet the average consumer does not have access to this service, as it tends not to work well until certain economies of scale are reached, and this is easier to achieve with high-net-worth individuals as clients. These offices can cost millions of dollars to run.

Alternatively, the financial experience advisor can create an alliance of partners who will fill the client's needs. It's not unlike the estate managers that high-net-worth people have here in Los Angeles to oversee maintenance, supervise staff members, and manage budgets and events. The marketplace is going to eventually demand a concierge-type service in the financial services world. The financial experience advisor, with his or her network of professionals, can step in with a sort of pseudo-family office, to efficiently take care of people today.

WHAT IS A FINANCIAL EXPERIENCE, ANYWAY?

You hear me mentioning *financial experience* a lot in this book. I define the financial experience as the participation in or direct observation of past financial events as a basis of knowledge and awareness moving forward. We use our past financial understanding to guide our current financial decisions to create our financially desired future; this past, present, and future make up the entirety of our financial experience.

We do not have a choice as to whether or not we will have a financial experience: by being alive on Planet Earth, we automatically have a financial experience. Whether we have to labor many hours to cover our cost of living or we were born into a generous trust fund, we need money for food, clothes, shelter, transportation, and anything else we require. There are bills to pay, health care costs to cover, and retirement years to plan for. If we are lucky, we may be able to save and invest.

As we move through life and make, spend, invest, and save money, our financial experience unfolds. Having a financial experience is unavoidable, but we can do much to affect the quality of our financial experience. Is it stable or risky? Is it reliable or stressful? Is it manageable or overwhelming? When financial experience advisors and atlas clients work together, they create a partnership to develop the kind of financial experience that the client seeks. Clients need to be clear about their goals for their financial experience advisors to be most helpful.

The following are examples of goals and preferences a client might have that a financial experience advisor would need to know:

- "I would like to invest aggressively to maximize my earnings and provide startup funds for businesses and projects."
- "I would like to be able to retire by age 55. I am willing to work as hard as I need to do it, as long as I can take the occasional vacation and live in a beautiful home."
- "I don't need a lot of things, but I want to have enough money to travel several times a year and live debt free."
- "I want to build a dream home without taking on any debt."
- "I'd like to leave an inheritance for my children and my children's children."

In the same way a doctor can't treat an illness a patient won't admit to having, a financial experience advisor needs to know what a client wants to accomplish to set the client on the path to success. As with many things in life, communication is key. Honest communication, a relationship built on trust, and a willingness to do the work necessary to achieve the established goals are all that is needed to set this financial team of advisor and client on the road to success.

In the same way a doctor can't treat an illness a patient won't admit to having, a financial experience advisor needs to know what a client wants to accomplish to set the client on the path to success.

An experience is the moment-to-moment awareness of internal and external events or a sum of events. It is time to let go of the idea that awareness is something to strive for—the end goal. Think of it as more of a way to get your feet wet. It is the beginning of acceptance. A financial experience involves accepting the challenges that come along with it, because you'll find that true financial freedom manifests itself at the locale of optimal challenge.

So how do we find the locale of optimal challenge? Let's say you want to set some goals for yourself. They're remarkable goals, but they're unattainable. You may find it frustrating and painful to pursue them, so you abandon them. Then you say, "Well, here's a goal," but you think, "I could do that standing on my head; there's no challenge in it." You may abandon that, as well, as it doesn't keep you engaged. Both extremes are going to leave you in a state that isn't characterized by the optimization of challenge in your financial life. One is too difficult, the other is too easy.

Therefore, what is the perfect prescription for maximum financial experience? First, take stock of where you are now. You might be taking on more pain regarding your financial situation than you are comfortable with. Alternatively, you might be in a place where your financial life feels stagnant—where you lack risk or direction. Your optimal financial challenge may begin by you either reducing or increasing the responsibility and pain points until they are tolerable or interesting enough to engage you. You don't have to fix everything at once. You could start by fixing just the things that you can manage today.

This is the main job of the financial experience advisor. He or she adjusts all the individual dials of comfort and discomfort to places that ensure you will stick with the plan. Without these adjustments, many people would quit before the miracle happens. Others, being aware that changes need to be made but unwilling to address them, don't even begin. Consumers want a financial plan they can hold to, engage with, and get excited about, and it helps to have someone to nudge them back on the path when they start to stray. Another term for a financial experience advisor could be a *stick-to-itiveness coach*. Whatever you call them, they are there to help you dial in a plan you will stick with and fully experience.

A MORE AFFLUENT SOCIETY: THE ROLE OF FINANCIAL EXPERIENCE ADVISORS IN THE CROSSOVER

Affluence has been on the rise in America. In 1971, 14.0 percent of Americans were designated *upper income* according to Pew research; by 2015, that percentage had risen to 21.1 percent.[7] Some of the most affluent people in the world are the most anxious. They are friendly people, with everything going for them, and yet they seem to be worried and agitated about everything. They have way more money than they can spend, but being well-off financially hasn't made them happy. This reflects one of the dominant moods during the crossover from an industrial to a tech-based economy and society: the new-found level of wealth seems to increase skepticism and decrease well-being, which is quite counterintuitive. History would tell us that everything we live with—including easy access to food, electricity, and plumbing—will all cease to work at some point; affluence seems to bring on the feeling, consciously and subconsciously, that the other shoe is about to drop.

A group of studies by Luthar, described in the *Monitor on Psychology*, indicated that suburban teens from families with an average annual income of $120,000 reported more anxiety, depression, and substance abuse than did adolescents from any other socioeconomic bracket. "'Families living in poverty face enormous challenges,' says Luthar, who has also studied mental health among low-income children. 'But we can't assume that things are serene at the other end.'"[8] This is not just a US issue: a World Health Organization study looking at almost ninety thousand individuals across five continents and eighteen countries found that those in more affluent countries experienced more depression.[9]

People have never been more financially successful or more anxious about that success than they are right now in the Specialization Age. And lest we assume that only upper income Americans have to consider these issues, let's not forget that on an absolute basis, people in the United States are quite wealthy. The average poor person in the United States, as defined by the government, has a place to live, a car to drive, food to eat, appliances to cook with, and entertainment options like TV and cable.[10] The living conditions of the average poor person should not be taken to mean that poor Americans live without hardship. But even a subset of lower-income individuals may feel they have something to lose in the Specialization Age.

The more it becomes possible for people to increase their incomes and assets, the less secure many of them feel about the technologically driven world that is making this possible. Affluence forces people to make challenging and painful decisions about how to allocate their resources in a world with even more options. People also often wonder what they have done to deserve the affluence that so many of their ancestors were never able to experience. They fear that the pressure to preserve and expand their material wealth is causing them to neglect their spiritual and emotional health.

I believe that the anxiety caused by increased affluence offers an opportunity for atlas clients to be extraordinarily impactful in the Specialization Age. Put simply, the more anxiety there is, the more opportunity there is for well-intentioned planning led by an advisor, which in turn can inspire the confidence and capability of tens of millions of individuals who are living in a society where many influential people are otherwise obsessed with bad news.

The anxiety is real. The solution that the financial experience advisor presents is real, as well.

FINANCIAL SHOPPING WITHOUT A PLAN

Most people I know handle their financial lives in a way I call the *shopping cart approach*: Every now and then, something catches their eye, so they pick up a new mutual fund here, and a new bank account there, and a life insurance policy from a third vendor. These may be legitimately good purchases, but your financial holdings should be part of a coordinated effort rather than a series of independent decisions.

When people approach financial products this way, they have essentially created a hodgepodge of investments without considering how each investment fits within their overall plan. It's not unlike going to the grocery store without a list: The bags you walk out of the store with may be filled with nice individual items, but chances are you won't have everything you need to cook a gourmet meal. If you don't want to run back to the store later, you need to figure out what you want ahead of time, write it down, and then seek it out. This is true for meal planning, which is a relatively straightforward task. Financial planning is clearly more complex—so why would we think it's OK to throw into our shopping cart whatever hits our fancy on any given day, without a holistic plan or more coordinated effort?

Often what you need before you even go to the store is some help in figuring out what you want to make and then what you need to make it. Given that this is the Specialization Age and plenty of help is available for planning your meals and shopping list (with services like Relish!)—or you can even have your shopping done for you via Peapod or Blue Apron—doesn't it seem like you should be able to get similarly specific help in creating and pursuing your financial goals? *What if, in a ninety-minute meeting, you could flesh out your desired financial future and be able to succinctly communicate to your advisor what pains you, what makes you feel good, what goals you want to accomplish, and what you value, so your financial experience advisor could craft a financial experience you will stick with? Wouldn't that be a service worth seeking out?*

So far, I have shown that there's a need for a greater degree of individualized service in the financial industry, and financial experience advisors are just the professionals to meet that need.

- Financial experience advisors will identify the emerging needs of individuals in a world of unpredictable change.
- It is the financial experience advisors who will innovate new forms of service and support that enable millions of people to gain greater direction, confidence, and capability in their lives and businesses.
- Moreover, it is the financial experience advisors who will transform their innovations into educational systems that make it

possible for thousands of other advisors to master these new forms of value creation.

- Financial experience advisors will also make enduring social contributions. Financial experience advisors will arrive at innovative social solutions in many areas where governments have failed. They will enable millions of people to become more productive economic citizens and to use their resources in more socially empowering ways.

I recognize that these are ambitious claims, but this is an ambitious book. Most important, the facts speak for themselves; they are quite obvious for those who have ever bothered to read the handwriting on the subway walls and tenement halls.

CONCLUSION: FINANCIAL CUSTOMIZATION IN THE AGE OF SPECIALIZATION

In the Specialization Age, the traditional financial advisor is not aging well. Consumers want all of their experiences, including their financial experiences, personalized to fit their own goals, means, and compromises. When it comes to building wealth, they want to partner with someone who can create a financial plan specific to their own situation and meet it, even if it means deploying a team of professionals to make sure all the items on the checklist get done. They also know that they need to remain engaged in the experience if things are to work out exactly as they want them to. What consumers need is a financial experience advisor. How do they find one? Read on to learn what someone in the market for a financial experience advisor should look for.

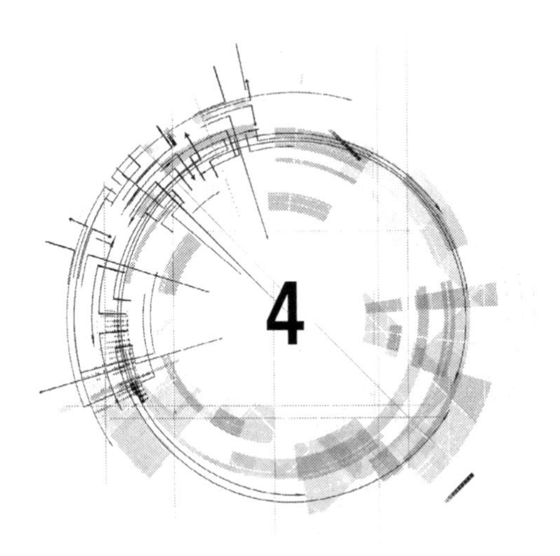

Choosing Your Course: Rent or Buy?

Life always offers you a choice. Paper or plastic? Fries or salad? The financial planning and investment management industry is no different. Having spent more than a decade in the trenches, I have observed financial choices from two extremes as lived out in clients who have collected investments from product sellers and those who have insisted on a holistic plan. In some cases, a product works perfectly well for a client. In other cases, some things fit and others don't. What I never saw was one approach that would work for all people. This is why it's important to find a financial experience advisor who is right for you and your needs. This advisor will understand your vision and will want to see your plans come to fruition just as sincerely as you do.

That got me thinking. The world is not at all black and white, and the range of services offered by financial advisors is broad. Some of the services are anchored by professional designations like the CFP® (CERTIFIED FINANCIAL PLANNER™), and, for companies, RIA (Registered Investment Advisor). A person who works for an RIA is an IAR (Investment Advisor Representative). Although there isn't a Financial Experience Advisor designation available (yet!) to explicitly define the requirements of the position, certain critical characteristics must be present for an advisor to be considered one.

As I have discussed, though, the primary focus of the financial experience advisor would be on the quality of the overall financial experience versus the quantity of the products sold or commissions earned. For too long, the industry has been shaped by the sales mentality. I can tell you that behind the scenes, the drive to push product out the door was obvious in everything from training sessions for new advisors to compensation formulas. If you could not generate the required sales volume as an advisor, you were deemed a failure.

This created a certain wirehouse mentality: sell stuff first, build relationships later, if you get to them. Because of the compensation structure and the pressure to fulfill the first imperative (i.e., sell stuff), these transactional advisors could only afford to see the person behind the checkbook after the sale was done. (If that sounds a little backward to you, I agree.) With no true relationship or connection to fall back on, the advisors were forced to sell commoditized products and, in so doing, inadvertently turned the clients themselves into faceless commodities.

I am not saying that everyone employed by a wirehouse is a heartless used car salesman. Far from it! The majority of people who work in wirehouses are well-trained professionals and good humans. However, there is no denying that the system was built to measure and reward signing bonuses, commissions, the size of your book of clients, and your ability to sell "flavor-of-the-month" products. The pressure is unavoidable and gets to the best of us. Clients lose out because of the inevitable conflicts of interest that this environment breeds. Advisors become like the tail wagging the dog, when the client should be the one who decides what gets his or her tail wagging.

For financial experience advisors, relationships create the foundation that allows them to deliver a valuable service.

To be sure, new clients are very important to any financial practice. Advisors need to eat and buy their kids soccer uniforms and braces, and to do that, they must get paid. However, just because something is intangible (like a connection, depth of planning, or a timely coaching session about a money decision) does not mean it has no value. For financial experience advisors, relationships create the foundation that allows them to deliver a valuable service. Business growth follows naturally; critically, so too does long-term stability.

As someone who was a part of the wirehouse workforce once upon a time, I have come to view selling products as training for something deeper and more valuable. The state of the industry at the time I entered it forced me to confront the disconnect between selling a product and offering a fiduciary service—that is, a service with the client's best interest in mind. I knew the product-first approach worked well for certain clients. I just wanted to have an opportunity to build the relationship first, because I knew that the only way I could truly help clients build up was by first building down. The foundation is the most important part of any relationship. What if a great service experience and human connection could be a default starting point rather than a luxury?

Which brings me to my current choice of employer. Today, I am a part of an RIA team that gives me the freedom to be an advocate for my clients. This framework allows me to be more creative and connected to the people who trust me with their money. As a wirehouse broker, I would be pressured to leverage the preset platform provided; as an RIA, I can shop around for best-in-class solutions in all categories, which translates into more options and better prices for clients. RIAs are well-regulated to protect investors, but the rule book is also better aligned with the way I work. In the RIA space, advice is separated from asset custody and product manufacturing—a benefit to clients because it eliminates conflicts of interest and allows the advisor to act as a true fiduciary.

What if a great service experience and human connection could be a default starting point rather than a luxury?

I chose to walk away from a wirehouse and join a practice that emphasizes a focus on the long-term, human connection and fiduciary responsibility to the client. So we are back to choice, aren't we? As an atlas investor, you, too, have choices in front of you. Out of the dozen names in your local phone book, which advisor is best for you? What are the pros and cons of working with a traditional financial advisor (i.e., a transactional broker) versus a financial experience advisor (i.e., a relationship-focused advisor)?

This is not all that different from making a decision to buy a house or rent an apartment. On the one hand, not everyone is in a position where buying a house makes sense right now. On the other hand, renting an apartment forever is not right for everyone, either. A wide range of housing options are available, so you can find what's right for you at any given life phase or set of circumstances.

Where does this comparison leave us? Believe it or not, yes, I'm saying that it's OK for some people to keep collecting financial products by working with a traditional financial advisor, and others should consider taking the plunge and working with someone who has an approach that is more like that of a financial experience advisor. What type of advisor an individual should work with depends on an individual's personal set of circumstances. One should not work with a financial experience advisor until one is truly ready to do so. This is because you must be ready to make a commitment to your long-term financial success to optimize the outcomes of a financial experience advisor's services. This takes a level of maturity, and I never, ever endorse the forcing of maturity. It simply doesn't work. I only advocate for those who are willing to take some responsibility for the process to join forces with a financial experience advisor.

What does it look like to take on responsibility—to be an atlas client? It means caring for your own financial household in the same way that you would tend to someone you really cared about, like a friend in need, a sick child, or an aging parent. You wouldn't skip a lunch date with a friend in crisis, keep medicine from a sick child, or leave an aging parent in bed without care. You would be willing to put in time and effort to make sure the person you cared about would be OK. If you are ready to be an atlas client, you are willing to give that same care to yourself; you are committed to being part of your own rescue. You are willing to take a fair inventory of yourself and your finances so you can work with your advisor to meet your financial goals. You are able to stop tricking yourself into believing everything will magically be all right when it comes time to pay for college or retire, and you will work with your advisor to design a realistic plan and stick to it.

As an empowered atlas client, you are also willing to be completely transparent with your advisor—about your financial situation, your assets and your debts, your strengths and your weaknesses, your income, your job stability, your risk tolerance, and more—so that your advisor has all the information he or she needs to support you. This is a problem I see consistently—clients picking and choosing what they tell advisors—and this selective sharing of information handicaps advisors, making it nearly impossible for them to provide fully effective counsel and holistic financial planning. How can your advisor give you good advice if you don't share that your job is on the rocks, you hide the fact that you have $50,000 in credit card debt, or you withhold personal financial goals?

Most of us are not comfortable disclosing our complete lifestyle and finances to a stranger, but guess what? Your advisor should not be a stranger or even an acquaintance. You need to develop a real relationship with your advisor (for tips, see the text box "Nine Ways You Can Deepen the Bond between You and Your Financial Advisor" in Chapter 6). Invest time in having conversations, talk about life philosophies and your families, have meals together, invite your advisor to your home, and accept invitations from your advisor to attend outings together. Relationships require good communication and time spent together. (If your advisor is not interested in developing a relationship, that's your clue to move on.) This is what I mean when I say *responsibility*. Are you willing to be an atlas client—to take responsibility for building the strength of your own financial household? If so, read on.

Here are five questions to ask potential advisors as you consider which advisor is the best fit for you (see Figure 4.1). Although the financial experience advisor designation does not yet exist, I am hopeful that books like this one will inspire efforts that will lead to the creation of a name and designation for this kind of advisor in time. In the meantime, use the questions and tips in the chapter to guide your search for an advisor who approaches the financial experience advisor ideal.

Figure 4.1: Five Questions to Ask when Hiring a Financial Advisor

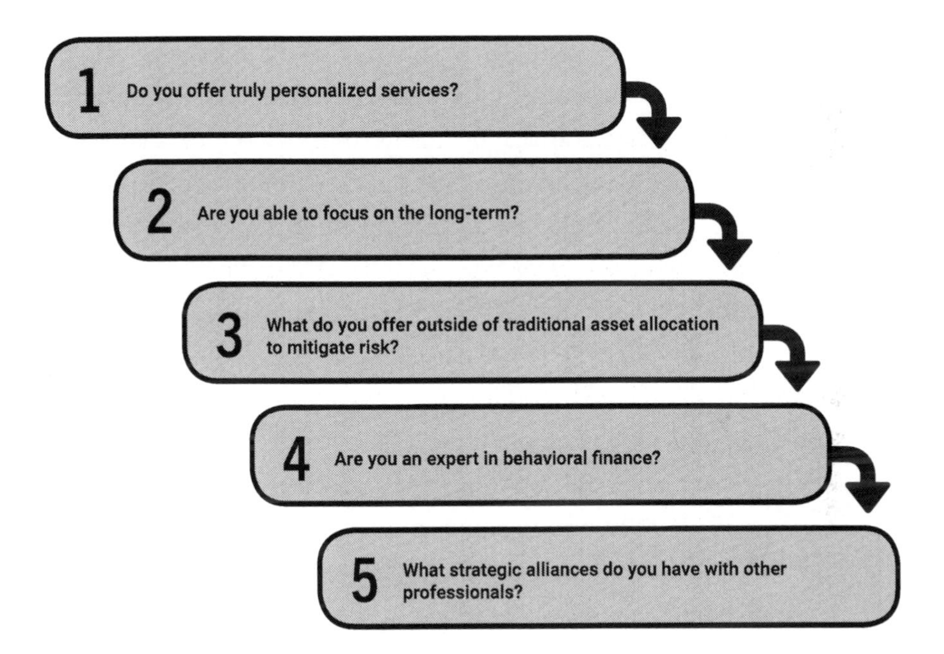

QUESTION 1: DO YOU OFFER TRULY PERSONALIZED SERVICES?

The new interconnected global economy is all about individualization of experience. Imagine you buy a ticket to a theme park. You walk in and find that every ride you take is tailored to the experience you want to have. This is how I envision the Specialization Age: everything is personalized.

As we move further through the Information Age and into the Specialization Age, economic breakthroughs in the global economy are being found increasingly in the area of unique consumer experiences. This can be seen most clearly right now in the hospitality, transportation, and entertainment industries. However, the concept of unique customer experiences is quickly taking hold in other industries. The reason is simple: Individuals will pay a premium for an experience that keeps them from being treated like a commodity. As large corporations commoditize more and more of the necessities of everyday life, people are increasingly open to unique, memorable, and motivating experiences provided by entrepreneurs in all fields. In addition, the more such experiences are available to them in one area of life, the more that people come to expect this personalization in other areas of life.

What I have described so far represents a very different way for advisors to approach the marketplace. Instead of selling commoditized products or services, financial experience advisors are offering a unique thinking-and-planning experience. The important word here is *experience*. An experience is the opposite of a commodity. To determine clients' needs, an advisor must go far beyond specific asset management or estate planning requirements and into the realm of their most important values, relationships, and lifelong dreams. Uncovering these is the critical skill that the advisor brings to the table. Nearly all financial advisors use some type of fact-finding process when first meeting with clients or prospective clients. However, these questions usually focus on assets and net worth and do relatively little to uncover who the clients really are. In contrast, the financial experience advisor will delve into many categories—only one of which concerns assets—to help ensure that the financial experience advisor has an intimate understanding of the client and what his or her individual needs may be.

Given the need for personalization—or what might be called *individualization*—financial experience advisors save the sale of products for the implementation stage of the financial plan. That is, financial experience advisors use financial products to implement solutions that are designed in the course of their conversations with clients. These implementations always occur at the end of the process, after a robust trust relationship has been established between the advisor and client. This means that financial experience advisors never sell products based on price and do not have to explain why a product has been recommended, because that product is filling a discussed need. It also means that the products they choose are only those that best bring about the transformative solutions needed by the client, as revealed in the financial experience.

Financial experience advisors never sell products based on price and do not have to explain why a product has been recommended, because that product is filling a discussed need.

I am reminded of a story of a woman who lost her husband and continued to trust his longtime financial advisor to help her take care of her family. Unfortunately, the trust was misplaced. The advisor did not adjust his aggressive approach to buying and selling stocks approved by her late husband to reflect the needs of a widow without a job who was raising small children. The trading fees and losses had piled up, and she was under a lot of unnecessary stress in her time of mourning. If her husband's advisor had looked at the big picture and adjusted her financial plan to meet her family's current needs, she could have saved a lot of money. If he had explained the implications of her husband's choices, she would have had an opportunity to make more informed decisions. A financial experience advisor would have allocated her remaining assets less aggressively, updated her insurance policies to protect her children, and had conversations with her to provide her with a new sense of financial control and well-being, all while offering clear explanations to help her make better decisions and dropping the advanced financial jargon so that she could make sense of her options more easily.

Choosing a Financial Experience Advisor Tip 1: *When choosing a financial experience advisor, make sure that the advisor takes time to get know every detail of your situation that you are willing to divulge. You can't just go to a doctor and say "make me healthy" without answering questions about your current lifestyle and your family history, submitting to measurements of your temperature and blood pressure, and so on. Moreover, would you trust a doctor that looked you up and down and gave you a clean bill of health?*

QUESTION 2: ARE YOU ABLE TO FOCUS ON THE LONG TERM?

Anyone who has ever attempted to save money knows that delaying gratification is tough. The future is such an abstract concept that humans have a difficult time prioritizing their future needs over what's urgent and shiny today. For example, would you rather splurge on the bigger and better new car you crave today or buy the more sedate used vehicle that will reliably get you around town so you can put the rest of said money into your retirement or college savings account? Oh, so fun! versus b-o-r-i-n-g! Or maybe the choice you're trying to make is whether you should spend time optimizing your credit card points or sit around watching TV. One choice is endlessly complicated, and the other is very easy, and don't you deserve some down time?

The financial experience advisor will help you focus on your own long-term financial picture, because he or she is not incentivized to counsel you to lock in the short-term wins that gain him or her a high commission now rather than putting you in products that ensure your financial growth fifteen years from now, when he or she has moved on to a new firm or retired. In financial planning, this translates into having hard conversations and forgoing some short-term rewards in favor of a solid long-term strategy.

What allows financial experience advisors to focus on the long term is that they are paid up front for their financial experience.

What allows financial experience advisors to focus on the long term is that they are paid up front for their financial experience. One of the greatest sources of freedom in the financial experience approach comes from advisors receiving an advance payment. Every advisor brings a wealth of wisdom to his or her interactions with clients, but far too often, traditional financial advisors treat this knowledge as an intangible value add-on that can help the advisor win a product sale rather than a skill that can be used to address unique client concerns. The advisor gives the knowledge away for free and stakes his or her compensation on the outcome of the product sale. In contrast, financial experience advisors are always paid up-front fees for the value they create. Clients commit to the process by writing a check. The size of these checks increases as advisors gain problem-solving experience and a positive reputation. When additional problem-solving tools are added to a financial experience, the client is billed for these accordingly.

Another way to look at this is that a traditional financial advisor who does not have a deep relationship with the client cannot afford to have a bad quarter. The client and advisor have not established a strong relationship over the goals they have discussed in depth and are working toward as a team. Rather, the advisor is disposable; if the advisor is not accomplishing what the client was hoping to achieve, even if those goals were not explicitly stated, the client can easily leave this advisor and find another one (who perhaps will have the psychic ability to divine what it is the client wishes to accomplish financially).

Neither can the advisor confront a client about a decision to buy a third vacation home instead of meeting critical savings goals. The relationship the traditional financial advisor has is based on the product the advisor is trying to sell. Bad financial decisions on the part of the client cannot be addressed: The advisor doesn't know whether the third vacation home will derail the client's progress toward his or her financial goals, because the advisor doesn't know what these goals even are. Maybe the client ultimately wants to run a bed-and-breakfast, and in that light the purchase makes perfect sense, rather than the home appearing to be yet another financial albatross the advisor needs to work around to sell his or her own high-commission products. The point is, the advisor doesn't know for sure what the home represents, because the advisor and client have not established what the client wants to accomplish; their only certainty is that the advisor is selling something that the client may want to buy.

To put it bluntly, a long-term advisor can afford to push the client to make hard decisions that are in that client's best interests.

To put it bluntly, a long-term advisor can afford to push the client to make hard decisions that are in that client's best interests. The advisor is not delivering rainbows and unicorns, just a healthy dose of truth along with a lot of compassion.

The true value of financial advice is in encouraging consistent saving and investing behaviors, not picking a couple of winning stocks once. You cannot plan on lucking into a few investments that create lasting financial freedom, no matter how much you want to. Picking a financial product or two here and there won't do the trick, either. You must start with a holistic overview of your goals, resources, and needs, then use them to create a strategy that is executed judiciously and consistently over years, while adjusting for changes in your life circumstances. If your advisor only gets paid when he or she sells you something, this approach is unsustainable: either you will be enticed to buy things you don't actually need, or your advisor will drop you as a client.

Financial experience advisors are able to focus on your whole financial picture, now and in the future, because the way they keep you on as a client is by building, brick by brick, a financial structure that will protect you and your assets, executing a plan that the two of you have discussed and agreed on. The experience is less the razzle-dazzle of Vegas—The lights! The sounds! The fast talking! The persuasive logic that the last roll of the dice didn't work out, but we were so close, let's try that just one more time—than the comfort of, well, whatever makes you comfortable! You and your long-term advisor have mutually established what you're trying to do and are working together toward a goal. If you're on the journey together and you both are fully invested in the outcome, neither one of you is likely to change horses midstream.

Choosing a Financial Experience Advisor Tip 2: *Make sure your advisor is set up to help you successfully manage your financial picture for the long term. Signs that your partnership is properly designed and incentivized for the long term include the following:*

- Your advisor gets paid based on a percentage of your net worth, a flat fee, or a fee for hours of service provided, not by commissions on investments purchased.
- Your advisor communicates with the entire advisory team rather than making solo moves in silos he or she is not entirely familiar with.
- Your advisor keeps you updated on progress and checks in occasionally to see whether your life situation or goals have changed so that the financial strategy can be adjusted accordingly.

FINDING AN ADVISOR FOR THE LONG TERM

Let's be honest: building a long-term relationship with an advisor requires an investment of time and a strong commitment. I think of it in terms of three components: the right client, the right advisor, and the right time. I am not the right advisor for every qualified prospective client out there right now, and that is OK. No advisor is. How can you choose the right advisor for you? Here are some filters to get you started.

Think about your needs over your lifetime, not just today. A long-term collaboration means that you are choosing a professional today whom you hope will be the right one to help you for years to come. There are extraordinary advisors out there who have deep expertise in half a dozen areas that you will require assistance with now and in twenty years. Others have assembled into teams of experts with a broad range of competencies. This range is more important than you may appreciate if you're focused only on what you need right now. But consider this: Although your current job may not have the most extraordinary paycheck, what do you project your income to be in five, ten, fifteen years? You may not have dependents today, but do you hope to have them in a decade? You may not own a house at the moment, but do you want to in the foreseeable future? If you can picture needing to consult with an expert in value investing, 529 plans, or mortgages in the future, then make sure an advisor or advisors with those specialties are on your team now.

Look for an external support network. No matter what your life situation is today, chances are you are going to need a great CPA or attorney at some point over the next decade or two. Look for an advisor with a world-class professional network. Some can even connect their clients with the perfect realtor or orthopedic surgeon if need be! An advisor who is well-known and respected in the professional community is a fantastic asset to you in the long run.

Consider hiring a multigenerational practice. Picture yourself in a prospect meeting. You have met with the advisor three times so far, and he seems really experienced and knowledgeable—and a head of gray hair reinforces the point that he's got plenty of experience at his fingertips. But if that advisor is telling you that he will work tirelessly to get you to your perfect retirement, how can you trust that statement? It is obvious that he will retire before you do! This is a good time to ask about the structure of his practice. What is his succession plan? Are there young advisors being trained and groomed to take over your portfolio as he steps away from the business? If this older financial advisor has a younger partner or team trained to approach financial planning using his relationship-based approach rather than a product approach, expect to include others in your planning meetings and rest easy knowing that, indeed, this advisor is laying the groundwork to meet your needs well into the future.

QUESTION 3: WHAT DO YOU OFFER OUTSIDE OF TRADITIONAL ASSET ALLOCATION TO MITIGATE RISK?

In the Information Age, asset classes became more highly correlated, meaning they no longer behave as differently from each other as they used to. As a result, just allocating your assets between classes does not produce the benefits it once did. Because news travels fast in the Information Age and we are all linked together, Asian markets affect US markets and vice versa; stocks from one industry may not perform that much differently from stocks in a different industry. Even real estate, which was once considered a great way to hedge one's stock market investments, tends to follow the same highs and lows of the market. So in the Specialization Age, attaining the safety that diversification has been historically expected to achieve is not as easy as it used to be. Nowadays, to build the wealth you need while working within acceptable risk margins, you must not only diversify your assets but also expand your strategies.

Traditional financial advisors tend to use one strategy: bet on the stock market. They will cloak this strategy in the framework of diversification by helping you invest in stocks and/or mutual funds from different sectors, countries or regions, and industries and throwing in some bonds for a splash of low but stable return. But as I have said, this kind of diversification in today's global era is no longer truly diverse. Losses caused by market volatility in one slice of your investments are supposed to be offset by hedges, but when the hedges start reacting to market conditions like the volatile assets do, you have a big problem.

Also keep in mind that, relatively speaking, the stock market has not been that volatile since 2000 (apart, of course, from the volatility experienced in 2008–2009), perhaps due to the tech boom, and it may not be representative of what's to come. This relatively calm stasis that many of us have gotten used to over the past two decades is likely not sustainable.* Financial experience advisors understand that they must offer you additional strategies that protect you from the ups and downs in the stock market, creating a new kind of diversification for the Specialization Age.

Your logical next question may be: "Do I really have options besides investing in the stock market and/or instruments that are positively

* The rare combination of equity and bond prices falling at the same time has become more frequent as of late. Since 2000, there have been fifty-seven trading days where the S&P 500 lost 0.5 percent or more and the thirty-year US Treasury bond yield also rose three basis points or more (note that when bond yields rise, bond prices fall).

correlated to stock market returns such as bonds and commodities and real estate?" The answer is yes! In fact, I specifically design portfolios that use several of these alternate strategies to weather black swan events like the economic crisis of 2008. At least one of these strategies comes to mind—*merger arbitrage*—and I use it regularly with my clients with great success. This strategy involves investing in companies that are scheduled to merge in the future. Typically in such mergers, the acquiring company's stock prices go down while the acquired company's stock prices go up.

You might think that merger arbitrage is a risky move, but, in fact, returns are quite good with this strategy, because the stock-value dips and rises resulting from mergers are relatively predictable. The fund I designed using this strategy has had an average annual return rate of around 6 to 7 percent over the time period of 2003–2018.* The merger arbitrage strategy is not correlated with the stock market, which means it offers true diversification for the consumer. Why haven't you heard of merger arbitrage before? Because this strategy is typically used by large investment banks for corporate investing. In the Specialization Age, such strategies increasingly can be made accessible to the average consumer or investor. Otherwise, the next economic crisis will bring down investors, even more than during the last go-round in 2008, because investors are less and less diversified!

As a result, consumers need to start thinking like entrepreneurs for solutions to their issues; they need to be open to ideas and ready to pounce on the ones they like. However, to achieve this, they need advisors with the right mind-set, values, and services that align with the tenets of the

* Remember that past performance may not be indicative of future results; different types of investments involve varying degrees of risk; and there can be no assurance that the future performance of any specific investment, investment strategy, or product made reference to directly or indirectly in this book will be profitable, equal any corresponding indicated historical performance level(s), or be suitable for your portfolio.

new age. Consumers will also need financial experience that continually develops and grows as a force in the marketplace, affecting what they choose to invest in, the strategies they apply, and especially the advisors they hire and choose to heed. Advisors must be able to offer their clients truly diverse investing strategies, not just so-called diversification within traditional asset classes that have become correlated in a global marketplace. This will enable clients' financial experiences—regardless of what changes take place in society, in the economy, and within the financial services industry—to always remain relevant, effective, and adaptable.

Choosing a Financial Experience Advisor Tip 3: *If you ask an advisor, "What do you offer outside of traditional asset allocations to mitigate risk?" and the advisor doesn't have a good answer, that advisor probably does not have a robust enough investment strategy to protect you and your assets should the economy go south. (While financial experience advisors can be described as investor-centric rather than investment-centric, their ability to help you manage your investments is still key.) Mitigating drawdown (losses) should be your number one priority, as you can only grow what you protect and secure.*

QUESTION 4: ARE YOU AN EXPERT IN BEHAVIORAL FINANCE?

Financial advisors, in times past, had to build a relationship with their clients if they were to succeed. Today, they must go a step further and become a behavioral coach, offering clients the advice they need to make sound investment decisions.

When it comes to resisting temptation, our brains are simply not built to do so. In fact, as humans, we are generally terrible at making good money decisions. The list of common biases that afflict savers and investors is long. You have probably heard about *mental accounting*, or a tendency to separate your assets and liabilities into different mental accounts to explain your actions. There are also other biases, like *confirmation bias*, a tendency to notice factors and facts that match your worldview and ignore those that contradict it, and *familiarity bias*, a desire to invest in familiar assets. If biases are bad, shouldn't we just address them? Well, it is not that simple.

For one, turning off natural biases is not only impossible but also counterproductive. Biases help speed up our decision-making process.[1] Without them, making a choice between paper and plastic would take several minutes—or, by the time you decided to run out of the way of a speeding train, that train would be on top of you. In practical terms, our brains did not build the helpful bias shortcuts overnight. It takes a long time to reprogram those pathways.

The good news is that it is possible to get informed and reduce the negative influence of these biases on your investing and spending behaviors. Understanding and mastering our own biases should mean not only being aware of innate evolutionary impulses but also understanding how they manifest in social behavior. We like to think that we operate from internally coherent, ethical, social, and political frameworks. You don't. I don't. We don't. No one does. In other words, the more you know about thine own self, the more you are able to be true.

What is the best way to accomplish that? In my experience, it takes getting educated and partnering with a trusted advisor who is an expert in behavioral finance. *Behavioral finance* is a field of study that uses psychology to understand why people make certain money decisions, including those that are problematic or irrational.[2,3] The primary goal of behavioral finance is to help people make "optimal financial decisions and display sensible financial behavior."[4]

All investors have a problem, but it's not the market that they typically have a problem with—the problem is often coming from within themselves. What you should understand is that the human brain takes time when making decisions, but in the fast-paced world of Wall Street, decisions must be made quickly. Therefore, mistakes are made because humans are prone to making them. It's normal behavior. Many of the behavior functions people are born with have a purpose. Yet, in some situations, these innate behaviors are problematic. Whereas anxiety about being killed by a bear in the wild when a bear was nearby saved our ancestors from being eaten, anxiety about being killed by a "bear" market can cause human beings to sell low instead of holding through volatile markets and sell high.

When markets are volatile, it's more important to focus on managing behaviors than on picking certain investments.

When it comes to investments, people are selective in the information they pay more mind to, because they are overconfident in themselves and their beliefs. The difficult part isn't trying to determine what the price of a barrel of oil is or what the dollar is against the euro—anyone can figure that out with a quick Google search or the right software. The difficulty lies in the realization that fears and anxiety will play a part in the decision-making process, leading some to make bad decisions. When markets are volatile, it's more important to focus on managing behaviors than on picking certain investments. People generally have better results when working with a financial advisor, because the advisor knows his or her stuff and shares that expertise while coaching them.

It is imperative that financial advisors help clients to overcome their instinctive behavioral prejudices. Why? It will keep clients from making terrible investment choices that could hinder them from reaching goals they've set for themselves. A client is often his or her own worst financial enemy.

In 2018, the most effective financial advisors are behavioral coaches. In the past, giving investment advice was key to ensuring client success. Today, that's become commonplace, is available for free online, and is not as profitable for business. Instead, financial advisors must take a holistic approach with their clients and provide behavioral coaching to help clients meet their goals.

The basis for our judgments and opinions are usually the outputs of other compromised brains, processed through established cultural and social structures. The better you understand your own patterns and decision-making flaws, the more aware you will be of your urge to sell when the market dips or to buy as the market is rallying to historic highs. Your advisor is a critical influence keeping you grounded in your goals, accountable for your decisions, and cool under fire. When seeking a financial experience advisor rather than a traditional financial advisor, look for an advisor who has knowledge in the new and expanding field of behavioral finance. Some of the buzzwords of this field include *mental accounting*, *anchors*, *herd mentality*, *availability bias*, *confirmation bias*, *loss aversion*, *disposition effect*, *familiarity bias*, and *high self-rating*.[5]

Choosing a Financial Experience Advisor Tip 4: *Make sure your advisor has plenty of knowledge about behavioral finance—that is, the psychological reasons people make money decisions—and ways to keep a client on track. Signs that your advisor is knowledgeable in behavioral finance include:*

- A keen emphasis on helping you make good financial decisions through a rational, values-based approach
- A focus on preparing you for unplanned life events
- An understanding of how traditional financial practices are driven by psychology and neuroscience

QUESTION 5: WHAT STRATEGIC ALLIANCES DO YOU HAVE WITH CPAS, ATTORNEYS, AND INSURANCE PROFESSIONALS?

Although a financial experience advisor will be providing you with holistic financial planning, he or she can't execute every aspect of your financial plan. You will need an insurance provider to set you up with the right policy for your family, a good accountant to help you maximize tax savings, and attorneys to answer questions that may arise related to business, divorce, and other matters. Any advisor worth his or her salt should be able to rattle off an answer to this question fairly quickly, because the advisor should have existing relationships with these professionals. You don't want your advisor sending you cold contacts. You don't need someone to Google things for you; you want to work with people they already know, like, and trust and with whom they share a track record of successful outcomes. (For more insight on this topic, see the It's All about the Team section in Chapter 3.)

Choosing a Financial Experience Advisor Tip 5: *Make sure your advisor has a ready stable of respected professionals to connect you to. Signs that your advisor has a valuable network include the following:*

- In the course of tax planning, the advisor regularly consults with a particular CPA.
- While discussing advanced planning, the advisor mentions a trust and estates lawyer that has been good to work with.
- When talking about insurance, the advisor scans your policies and then sends them to a trusted specialist for review.

CONCLUSION: THE COMING ECONOMIC EVOLUTION

One way of looking at the current period of history is that the entire human race is in a fifty-year crash-course learning process, striving to master entirely new capabilities. Everybody on Earth is a willing or unwilling student in this school—financial advisors and consumers alike—and nobody can escape the lessons being taught. Everyone is continually being tested and graded. Those who pass their tests are promoted, and those who fail are held back until they are willing and able to learn. This period of planetary schooling may span the years from 1975 to 2025, after which a critical mass of the global population will be comfortable and confident with the demands and possibilities of the Specialization Age.

For me, *critical mass* means more than two billion individuals, worldwide, achieving personal daily success because of the advantages provided by tech-based tools, systems, processes, and networks. By 2025, everyone who was in a position of control and influence in 1975 will be dead or retired from active life. Most of the governmental mentality and methodology that still controlled society during the late period of the Industrial Revolution will have disappeared. The legislative leaders of 1975 will have been succeeded by individuals for whom operating in a tech-based economy and society feels like second nature. By that time, hundreds of millions of tech-friendly individuals will be found throughout all levels of society.

As the marketplace expands and discerning clients demand services to help them deal with the ever-increasing complexity of the world, there is a value in choosing an advisor who is comfortable with technology and open to ideas, regardless of their origin. Developments in genetics, artificial intelligence, and neurological research affect financial planning and investing. If you believe the solutions to your problems can only be found in familiar territory, you have fewer tools in the shed to choose from. Best-in-class financial advice will help you simplify your life and make better decisions. If your advisor is adding to the complexity and the noise around you, keep looking.

Every new financial experience is a creative amalgam of the clientele's fundamental concerns and issues and the advisor's life experience and wisdom as a problem solver.

The best advisors are those whose financial experiences were created and have evolved outside of corporate control. For this crop of advisors, every new financial experience is a creative amalgam of the clientele's fundamental concerns and issues and the advisor's life experience and wisdom as a problem solver. No other ingredients are required. The new breed of advisors consists of innovators, not duplicators. Most predict consumer demand rather than satisfying already existing demand in the market. This is problematic.

But why is this relevant? In the Specialization Age, asset classes are more highly correlated than they used to be. Global connectedness is one reason for this. It used to be that when something happened in one country, it did not affect other countries, or, if it ever did, it took quite a while to materialize. A political event in China did not necessarily affect the United States, and, if it did, it didn't happen overnight. However, global communication has evolved so rapidly over the past twenty-five years that worldwide events can now have an immediate effect on the US market. This instant global reactivity means that your portfolio now needs to be truly diversified to be ready for events that could occur at any time around the world, not just in the United States or on Wall Street. This requires a new kind of advisor who thinks creatively and is not beholden to old ways of investing.

Financial experience advisors believe that, through collaboration, the economic pie can keep getting bigger.

America is in a unique position. There's enough money, ingenuity, and heart in this country to make a difference to everyone in the world, so it's crazy to think in selfish, self-protective terms. The biggest problem in the United States is not scarcity of resources; rather, it's the lack of teamwork. Teamwork creates a bridge that helps to close the giving gap between wealthy individuals, advisors, and charities. Financial experience advisors believe that, through collaboration, the economic pie can keep getting bigger. They also believe that many different kinds of pies are being created by the tech evolution. The more pie makers we can bring to the buffet, the better the future will be for everyone.

The person you work with to maximize your piece of the economic pie and to figure out what you want to do with it needs to be attuned specifically to you and your needs. Before you get to work on your finances, you need to make a very careful decision about which financial experience advisor is going to accompany you on your wealth-building journey. You need someone who offers truly personalized services and who will be with you for the long haul. Your advisor needs to have plenty of insight into how to not only grow your wealth but also how to protect, through true diversification, what you have already gained. Finally, your financial experience advisor needs to be a coach who can help you to acknowledge hard truths and avoid the counterproductive money mistakes that people make in emotional or simply very human moments. The choice may not be easy, but your financial experience advisor is going to be your best friend and partner during the coming economic evolution, so choose wisely.

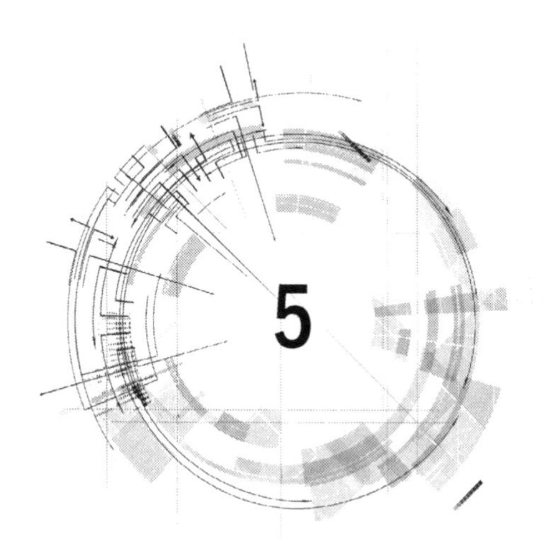

Atlas Now: Create Your Experience

When I was growing up in the Upper Midwest, a favorite family pastime was fishing. We would fish from the shore, from boats, and on the ice. Some of my favorite memories are going out with my dad or grandpa and throwing a line in to see what was biting. Looking back, I see how lucky I was to have these guys who orchestrated these fun mornings at the lake!

As I got older, I began to understand, more and more, that the fun of the day was very much dependent on the planning and preparation that was done before we headed out. I also started to be assigned fishing preparation tasks, such as packing the safety vests and cutting leeches on the lake. Fishing prep strategies began to become clear, too. Given that you need to be on the lake by sunrise (that's when the fish are biting, according to Grandpa), I realized that you want to hit the bait shop for your leeches, night crawlers, wax worms, or minnows the night before you fish. Speaking of bait, that needed to be chosen on the basis of what we were fishing for, how big we'd hope our fish would be, and what strategy we'd be using. I found that if you want to roll out of bed, grab the gear, and get to the water right after you wake up, it helps to have everything checked, prepped, and laid out so you can do just that once morning arrives.

Once I started fishing on my own, it dawned on me that that the experience of the day was dependent on *my* preparedness and not that of others. Luckily, the older generation had taken me fishing as a child, teaching me, from their own experience, how to get ready for a great day on the water.

Fishing is a lot simpler than managing your financial life, and yet both have this in common: your experience in either case is dependent on your own preparedness. First we must realize that we are the adults in charge of our own finances, so we must step into our power and take ownership.

I don't mean to state the obvious. I realize that if you are reading this book, you know you play an important role in creating your own financial success. What I really want to highlight is the importance of resisting the all-too-common urge to stick your head in the sand as a sort of defense mechanism against the overwhelming amount of information and choices raining down upon you in the Information and Specialization Ages, especially when it comes to finances. Financial management has gotten so complicated that many of us feel we have two choices: do nothing at all because we don't know where to begin or turn these duties over to a financial advisor or family member and disengage.

Well, my friends, we are at a time in human history when we need to take full responsibility for our own role in creating the financial experiences we desire, now and in the future. Do I believe that the guidance and support of a financial professional is essential? Absolutely. Today's complex world makes such support all the more important. (See the previous chapter, "Choosing your Course: Rent or Buy," for more information on choosing the right advisor for you.) Think of me as your Uncle Will with valuable wisdom to impart on how to be the boss of your own financial experience so that you can converse intelligently with your financial experience advisor and achieve your unique vision for the future. In this chapter, I provide a number of ideas for how you can empower yourself to take responsibility and adapt to change.

PAY OFF YOUR DEBTS

Before you start regularly saving and investing money, it is usually a good idea to pay down any debts you may have accumulated. Credit card debt, student debt, and even car loans can carry massive interest rates that drag you down and demand monthly payments that chip away at your revenue while racking up interest—and heaven forbid you pay late and incur penalties that take even more money from your future self. It's a relentlessly brutal cycle.

Don't let debt eat away at your potential; make paying off your debts as soon as possible a top priority. Also take a look at how you got into debt in the first place and do what it takes—reevaluate priorities, refinance, set up automatic payments, and so on—to make sure it doesn't happen again.

I use a special technique with clients that I learned from reading personal finance articles. The *debt avalanche* is a popular method of debt reduction recommended by many financial gurus. List your different loans, credit cards, medical bills, and other debts on a piece of paper or, even better, a computer spreadsheet. Make sure you include the remaining balance and interest rate of each debt next to its name. Only pay the minimums on all the low-interest debt and funnel any extra monies you have coming in toward paying down the balance carrying the highest interest. When you pay off that debt, apply that previous debt's payment to the next highest interest rate debt, and keep repeating this process until you are done.

Take heart! Once you take the difficult steps of beginning the wealth-building process—paying down your debt, establishing your credentials, building an investment portfolio, and so on—you will be setting yourself up for massive financial success later on.

THE REALITIES OF STAGNATION

The sad fact is that many people find themselves in the following situation:

> I just retired. I am seventy years old. I wish I had taken another career path, but I feel it is too late to do so now. I never learned or had the opportunity to learn how to build wealth with an endgame of being able to live off that fund of wealth. I am starting to feel the lifestyle creep of my choices over the past decades. I do not think this is sustainable. I watch the stock mar-

> ket every day with anxiety, knowing that I now have to depend on it—yet its gains and losses are outside of my control. My previous advisor did not seem to help or guide me to achieve my retirement goal, and I discovered too late that I paid way more in fees than I realized. What do I do if I want to build a fund to live off of and ensure my family is taken care of when I pass away? Whom do I trust? Can I do this on my own? How? How do I keep up with the changes?

How did we get to a point where most people have such little understanding and so little control over their own investments? Two things can be blamed for this. First, the industry was made too complex for individuals to manage their own investments. Second, the transfer of this essential life task to pros was made very easy.

This is exactly why new-age financial experience advisors are necessary: to guide you back to comprehensive control of your investments. For the evolving advisor, this is a second chance to shift from ethically questionable financial practices into being an advisor who offers financial experiences (not just services). This new position is not commission-centric but embodies a fulfilling, ethical, and social entrepreneurship approach centered on service and continual improvement versus status and job security.

The Information Age gave people greater access than ever to their finances, along with tools for educating themselves. I have found, though, that as consumers have gained access to more information, they have often felt the urge to run and hide from managing their financial experience, allowing unopened financial statements to pile up on the counter or in in-boxes and leaving voice mail messages from advisors unanswered. It hasn't helped that financial instruments and the overall marketplace have gotten more complex and that those running the financial industry tend to treat clients as if they are children incapable of understanding, much less managing, their finances. I believe such infantilization is unfair; many people are willing to take responsibility. Unfortunately, too often the answer to financial questions directed at traditional financial advisors is "Just trust us." Without enough knowledge to claim their own power, clients end up feeling helpless.

In the Specialization Age, the best of the past can be joined with the best of the present and the future when the guidance of financial experience advisors is tailored to atlas clients' personal financial needs through a cooperative, communicative relationship. Financial experience advisors will be the guides savvy enough to teach atlas clients how to successfully navigate the money strategies of a new age.

ECONOMIC MATURITY GAME THEORY

If you have picked up this book, it is likely you understand that expecting a retirement safety net to appear when you have not started weaving one is not a viable long-term strategy. This puts you one step ahead of most people. It's time, therefore, to stop procrastinating. Making decisions about saving and investing can be scary, but the longer you wait to get started, the fewer advantages you have.

I'd like to introduce you to something I call *economic maturity game theory*. Figure 5.1 illustrates the details of the four different types of people who play the game. These four groups vary on two dimensions: their expectation of having a financial safety net and their level of responsibility when it comes to money matters. There are those who expect to have a safety net and are very responsible but who have flawed perceptions of what an economic safety net might entail. Then there are those who do not expect a safety net and who take little responsibility while being aware that no one is going to swing in to save them in their old age, but they are also not taking steps to save themselves. Most people have a high expectation of having an economic safety net and are not doing much to put one in place themselves. The people we want to be are those who have a low expectation of a safety net (we can always be pleasantly surprised if one does appear, right?) but are taking responsibility for our financial lives. What square do you want to occupy in this game? No luck is required to land on your preferred square: the choice is entirely yours.

Figure 5.1: Economic Maturity Game Theory

Expectation of Safety Net	Overall Monetary Responsibility: Low	Overall Monetary Responsibility: High
High	Most people are here—the underlying thinking is flawed and personal risks are aplenty.	You were instilled with a value of responsibility during your upbringing yet have flawed perceptions today.
Low	Your understanding is correct, but you lack discipline or the ability to delegate.	The best place to be: You see the world as it is and respond and behave accordingly.

Most people live on autopilot. It is human nature to want to minimize the thought involved in making taxing decisions and use habitual pathways in our brain circuitry to save energy. That explains why we tend to eat the same thing for breakfast, use the same route to get to work, and buy the same brand of trash bags from the grocery store.

Unfortunately, the autopilot approach does not limit itself to helpful habits (like brushing your teeth and taking your multivitamin). When it comes to money, it's just as easy to get stuck in a rut. A few lucky people may have a rut that is incredibly constructive and works phenomenally well for them. The majority of us stumble into money habits by accident. Even the lucky ones that get it right in the beginning may eventually run into a life change that requires them to reassess how they handle things! Bottom line: if you are on money autopilot, you may as well realize it now so you can get back in the driver's seat and improve your financial experience not just for today but for tomorrow, when the seeds of today will be harvested.

Is there a test for that, you might ask? Why not?! Here is a helpful checklist of warning signs that you are not currently the boss of your financial experience. If you have a cluster of these indicators, you might not have as much control as you think you do. For some of you, this self-assessment may be one of the scarier parts of the book. I urge you not to skip it. Take a pen or pencil and check off any items on the list that apply to you often, most of the time, or always. If you are unable to do this part honestly and bravely, I am sad to say that the rest of the information in this chapter probably won't do you much good. If you find yourself hesitating, please take a deep breath and just jump in.

TEN SIGNS THAT YOU ARE NOT CURRENTLY THE ONE IN CHARGE OF YOUR MONEY

- ☐ You do not know how much total debt you owe.
- ☐ You use credit card checks or cash advances to pay your monthly bills.
- ☐ You associate saving with splurges and special purchases, not a savings account.

- ☐ You have a super-low risk tolerance (i.e., you are afraid to take any investment risk at all).
- ☐ You have a very high risk tolerance (i.e., you believe you are invincible and investment risk does not scare you at all).
- ☐ You have borrowed money from your 401(k) to help cover your monthly expenses.
- ☐ You have no budget and believe you don't need one.
- ☐ You have not reviewed and increased your 401(k) contribution since you took your current job.
- ☐ You are highly tuned in to and influenced by what other people are doing, saying, and spending money on.
- ☐ You are uncomfortable with the idea of discussing money with your significant other.

Was this checklist reassuring or disquieting? Would you prefer to rip this page out of the book, burn it, and pretend this assessment never happened? Here is the thing: Just as with health and nutrition, we tend to get a certain amount of leeway and grace in our younger years. As tested by generations of college students and fresh graduates, one can subsist on pizza and soda, party all night four nights a week, and ignore the idea of an annual physical exam when in one's late teens and early twenties. It may seem like your body will never break, but in reality, you are burning through your grace period.

Money is no different. Whether you are fortunate enough to have come from a family of means, had to build everything you have on your own, or experienced something between the two extremes, everyone's financial grace period has an expiration date. There may be a stretch when money seems easy or entirely out of your hands. However, at some point, you have to take charge and begin to make conscious decisions.

The good news is that you do not have to manage your financial life alone. In fact, the right trusted copilot can help you ensure your plane is sound, prevent you from veering off the runway, and guide you to the destination of your choice safely. That outcome, just like your decision to take a conscious approach to money decisions, won't happen by mere accident. Approach your decision about who should be your financial advisor with care and focus, because this person has the potential to make your life better (for more guidance, see the previous chapter, "Choosing Your Course: Rent or Buy?").

ADAPTING TO THE CHANGE

Consumer needs are shifting more quickly than ever and in more opaque ways. People have had so much financial information at their fingertips for so long that they need to ask themselves what kind of financial experience they want so they can home in on the information they actually need. The freedom to choose your own financial path is both empowering and frightening; a financial experience advisor can help you plan for the best but prepare for the worst. Remember, the market isn't always going to go up; you need a plan in place to preserve what you have so the market doesn't drag you down when it falls. For example, do you find the chance of having 50 percent more money in five years' worth the risk of having 50 percent less money in five years? If you take such a risk, the outcome is likely to be somewhere between those extremes, but it is the negative extreme that the prudent investor prepares for.

I believe that most, if not all, investors would answer that question with a resounding, "Going down by 50 percent is way, way worse than going up by 50 percent is good!" Research into loss aversion (that is, the sense that a loss is more painful than a gain is pleasurable, which leads to people going to greater lengths to avoid losses than to seek gains) supports that belief.[1] Managing the risk of loss is critical for investment success and peace of mind. Negative performance requires a larger percentage of returns than what was lost to break even. Therefore, using a trade strategy to limit losses to begin with could help increase performance potential by reducing the amount needed to recuperate should the investment go south. Your next logical questions probably are, in rapid succession, "How do I mitigate downside risk?" and "Isn't everyone and their mother trying to do that?"

The answer to the second question is yes. The answer to the first question lies in the following section. As a Registered Investment Advisor, I'm responsible for helping my clients achieve their investment goals. This is a responsibility that I take very seriously. Because it's important for all folks to have a basic understanding of the different strategies that can be used to manage their dollars, I encourage you to do your research and choose the strategy or strategies that make sense to you.

To that end, in this chapter, I outline what I believe financial experience advisors should be offering to their clients. I explain my trading methods and strategies, my overall investment philosophy, and why I believe my approach to investing will produce long-term successful results. This is where I really "geek out." I mean, I can spend eighteen hours a day looking at charts and building algorithms and not notice the passage of time. This is where golf comes in handy, as it gets me away from the computer screen, but I digress.

ACHIEVING GOALS IS GOOD; ACHIEVING GOALS WITH VISION IS EVEN BETTER

It's great to have goals, as they can help you to grow, be a better person, and have a better life. Goals without a vision—a reason for striving to achieve the goal—in contrast, are not as valuable. You must have a goal (e.g., I want to lose twenty pounds) and a vision to go with it (e.g., so I feel great at my new job or so I can live a long life and see my grandchildren), or else you risk not accomplishing anything.

The majority of people who set a goal without a vision can attain their goals but tend to have a negative view of the process. They just move onto the next goal they have once they cross one off the list; eventually, goal attainment begins to feel like a chore. Because there is not an overarching payoff or any meaning attached to the goal, they are not motivated to continue reaching goals. If you're going to attain goals and feel positive about your accomplishments, goals should be set in tandem with a vision. What are you looking to get out of the financial goals you set for yourself?

A look at what goals really are. What are goals? Alone, they are a particular target to attain. Collectively, they are the method you use to carry out the vision. Goals (e.g., I would like to save $40,000) should be set in conjunction with your vision (e.g., so I can have a beautiful wedding). If you have no vision, then meeting goals doesn't mean a whole lot. There is no "why" behind them to continually push you forward. Why bother creating goals if no bigger purpose is behind them?

Most people have financial goals such as the following:

- Save money
- Eliminate student loan and credit card debt
- Be your own boss
- Travel the world

Only sometimes are people conscious of having a larger vision that motivates the accomplishment of the goal.

A look at what a vision is. A vision gives your goals a "why." It gives you direction and a definition of the future you're looking to achieve. A vision involves your beliefs and core values and what you'd like your future to hold. It's the reason you do what you do—your purpose in life. A vision is your passion. It's something that keeps you motivated to continue what you're doing to attain the goals. It's inspiration.

No matter what goals you have—personal, business, or financial—your vision should be specific. Of course, for the more personal things in your life, your vision doesn't have to be very narrow. However, it still needs to be clear, so the foundation on which it's built remains firm.

How do you create a vision? First, identify your core values and passion. What do you believe is your purpose in life? How do you see your life going? Once you understand these things, then you can build and describe the vision your goal is designed to achieve.

The vision should encompass your values and how you want your future to be without being basic. Your vision can be adjusted as needed, such as when your overall situation changes. The idea is to have a vision that reminds you why you set goals in the first place and keeps you motivated. By having a vision, you'll be happier in achieving your goals, because you'll be able to observe your progress on the road to a bigger accomplishment.

Using the goals listed above, you can lay out a vision such as the following:

- To move your family to a safe community with great schools
- To free up money for things you want in life or to be a positive example for your kids
- To assist people in any capacity you can
- To be a student of the arts and culture

Creating your vision may seem like a difficult thing to do, but the effort you put into it is well worth it. You want to have a higher purpose when creating goals for yourself. You'll be happier for it.

I see the vision-based approach to wealth management as naturally evolving out of the goals-based approach, which evolved out of the traditional approach. Here's an overview of all three. Which approach do you feel will work best for you when you are working with a financial advisor?

- ***Traditional Approach:*** The focus is on individual financial products, one at a time, rather than together as part of a larger financial plan. If you have a vision, you don't know how everything fits into it because your advisor never asked you about your vision or set specific goals with you to realize it. You focus more on the market, choosing the product based on your risk profile, with attention on the benchmark performance and single-risk awareness. In the end, you wonder where you are now.
- ***Goals-Based Approach:*** Your advisor asks you what your financial goals are but does not ground these in a vision. Your advisor says she is creating a financial plan for you, but in the end, she still focuses on choosing products that are suitable, rather than providing consult as to what is in the best interest of you. You focus on progress toward the goals but take multiple undesirable risks in an effort to get to where you are going.
- ***Vision-Based Approach:*** Your advisor makes sure the financial vehicles you invest in are in line with not only your goals but also your vision. You focus on yourself, choosing products based on your values and vision and put attention on goals that match your vision. You mitigate the various risks and ask yourself, "How do I get there?"

With the traditional approach, you might say, "I would like to have more money." With the goals-based approach, you might say, "I want more money so I can buy a house." In the vision-based approach, you might say, "I want to live in a safe community with good schools so I can raise my family in it." See how they build on each other? They are interconnected, with ever-increasing opportunities for you to get clear on the "why" and the "what" behind the work you do with your financial advisor. Mindfully creating goals in pursuit of a vision with a higher purpose is the first step to achieving big results.

With the vision-based approach, you are moving toward a higher purpose and even a higher level of consciousness. It is the atlas shift in a nutshell. With responsibility comes purpose, and with purpose comes responsibility. If you want to be able to channel that purpose, use a vision-based approach. Finding purpose will bring you closer to happiness, and isn't that what we are all seeking in the end?

THE INVESTMENT PHILOSOPHY: BE DIFFERENT

In terms of my overall investment philosophy, I consider myself to be a chartist, among many other things. I wasn't always this way. I blame Roger Davis. He wrote a terrific book titled *Wall Street's Just Not That into You*,[2] where he dives into what I explain next, but in greater detail. This book is a must-read, especially if you have money in the market.

What is a chartist? The basic definition of a chartist is an individual who studies charts and graphs to understand the historical price levels of a particular stock, security, or market. A chartist then uses this information to forecast the stock's future price direction. More specifically, as a chartist, I am looking for certain price patterns in an effort to discover profitable trading opportunities. This particular investment philosophy can be implemented across all asset classes, including stocks, bonds, currencies, commodities, precious metals, and alternative assets.

My philosophy as a chartist is based on the premise that price movements in a security are not random but can be predicted through a study of past trends and other technical analyses. I've always thought that the more you work with the numbers and charts, the more the illusions of randomness begin to disappear. The financial advisors who say market movements are random or equate investing to gambling are the same people who have a vested interest in your buying their funds. Wall Street would rather you not know about these strategies.

As a wealth manager, my job is to address the important financial issues that my clients might encounter. One of those is the possibility of one, or more, stock market declines that are devastating. That's a risk, like it or not, and its one that's not prepared for most clients' portfolios.

CORE STRATEGY

In its simplest terms, the core strategy that most investors (whether they realize it or not) use to invest in the financial markets provides exposure to asset classes that broadly represent the overall market, like company stock within energy and technology or government bonds. The core strategy focuses on achieving expansive coverage with limited day-to-day management of the portfolio. Note that I'm talking about buying financial instruments and holding on to them, as opposed to day trading. You will probably find this strategy fairly familiar and straightforward. Its beauty lies in its simplicity.

A specific example of this core strategy would be an investment portfolio consisting of stocks and bonds. A popular ratio is usually a blend of 60 percent stocks and 40 percent bonds. Of course, these numbers can be adjusted on the basis of an investor's tolerance for risk, or the degree of variability in investment returns that an investor is willing to withstand.

Long-term historical results show that stocks have outperformed bonds on a rate-of-return basis. If stocks are such a great investment, why don't we remain 100 percent invested in stocks at all times? Because stocks are inherently more volatile than bonds; one rule of investing is that more risk equals more reward. They also have a tendency to generate periods of extended losing streaks in comparison to bonds. Over many time periods within the course of the past ninety years, stocks have performed rather poorly. For example, from September 1929 through July 1932, the stock market lost 90 percent of its value. It took twenty-five years for stocks to recover their losses from their peak in September 1929. More recently, the stock market fell 56 percent in 2009 during the financial crisis.

As investors, we don't have the luxury of waiting ninety years to fully capture the stock market's impressive average 10.2 percent annual rate of return.

Certainly, over the long run, stocks easily outperform bonds. However, as investors, we don't have the luxury of waiting ninety years to fully capture the stock market's impressive average 10.2 percent annual rate of return. Instead, most of us have an active investment career of approximately forty years. I argue later in this book (see Chapter 8,

"We Are All Living Longer") that atlas clients of today should be planning for unprecedented longevity. With that said, we have a finite time to capture return on our investments.

As I briefly discussed already, there are periods of time when stocks lose money and take several years to recover. Therefore, investors must diversify by adding bonds to their portfolio in an attempt to avoid the brutal losses that periodically occur in the stock market, or at least to have some padding to somewhat protect their nest egg.

On the surface, the core strategy (a mixture of stocks and bonds) appears to be sufficient to meet the needs of most investors. In fact, many investors spend their entire investment life cycle participating solely in the core strategy. I maintain that buy-and-hold can very well work on its own if you are in one of two situations: first, if you know when you're going to die, or second, if you're going to live forever. Unfortunately, most of us don't have either of these things going on.

Consequently, I believe you can generate better long-term results by adding to the core strategy. Therefore, in addition to the core strategy, I suggest an alternative strategy and a tactical strategy.

ALTERNATIVE STRATEGY

The objective of the alternative strategy is to incorporate an additional layer of diversification into the overall investment portfolio. This objective is achieved by investing in such things as merger arbitrage, commodities, and credit strategies. Most likely, many of you are probably unfamiliar with these investment vehicles because average retail investors generally have been relegated to traditional asset classes, and alternatives have been virtually unavailable to them—until recently. Keep reading to learn about each of these substrategies.

Merger arbitrage. As I discussed in the previous chapter, merger arbitrage involves simultaneously purchasing and selling the stocks of two merging companies. Essentially, this strategy speculates on the successful completion of mergers and acquisitions. Merger arbitrage is a type of "event-driven investing" that is an attempt to exploit pricing inefficiencies after a merger is announced but before it closes.

A merger begins when one company, the acquirer, makes an offer to purchase the shares of another company, known as the target. As compensation, the target company will receive cash at a specified price or the acquirer's stock at a specified ratio.

Merger arbitrage is a type of "event-driven investing" that is an attempt to exploit pricing inefficiencies after a merger is announced but before it closes.

There are two types of corporate mergers: cash and stock mergers. In a cash merger, the acquiring company purchases the target company's shares for cash. A stock merger involves the exchange of stock between the acquiring company and the target company. Cash deals are much preferred by those of us looking to benefit from the sale. Although the same transaction essentially occurs regardless of whether the deal is completed with a cash payment or with the purchase of a certain percentage of shares, there are often differences in the way in which the merger ultimately unfolds. Merger arbitrage managers take and manage risk in ways that are very different than others. The risk is shifted from market risk to deal risk. It's less important to a merger arbitrage manager the direction the market is going. What's important is the relationship between the performance of the acquiring company stock and the target company stock.

Commodities. I use commodities as a means to participate in an entirely different asset class than stocks. Commodities are one of the five major asset classes for investors and traders: stocks, bonds, real estate, commodities, and cash. Another name for this asset class, which refers to how money is made and directed, is *managed futures*.

What is a commodity? Quite simply, a commodity is a basic good used in commerce that is interchangeable with other commodities of the same type. Commodities are used in the production of other goods and services. Their most important feature is that there is very little differentiation between a commodity coming from one producer and the same commodity coming from another producer. For example, a bushel of wheat is basically the same commodity, regardless of the producer. This feature is what separates commodities from other goods and services.

Examples of commodities are wheat, corn, crude oil, cotton, gold, copper, sugar, cattle, cocoa, and natural gas. All of these commodities are traded on organized exchanges, which are very similar to a stock exchange. The largest exchange is the Chicago Board of Trade.

Commodities are particularly useful in a portfolio because they are not heavily correlated to stocks and bonds.

Commodities are particularly useful in a portfolio because they are not heavily correlated to stocks and bonds. In other words, these two asset classes generally don't move in the same direction. For example, during the past fifteen years (2002–2016), commodities have had a correlation with stocks of 0.32. That is, for every one-dollar move in a stock portfolio, a basket of commodities will move thirty-two cents in that same direction.

Credit strategies. My final suggested alternative strategy involves credit. This is a rather complicated investment approach. Therefore, I won't delve too deeply into the methodology.

A credit strategy is similar to merger arbitrage in the sense that it can be event-driven. However, that is where the similarities end, because merger arbitrage involves a company's stock, whereas credit strategies involve a company's debt (also known as *corporate bonds*).

In simple terms, investors who use credit strategies are searching for price differentials between various debt instruments issued by the same corporation. Companies issue debt instruments (i.e., bonds) to raise funds for their business operations. Investors who use credit strategies try to find relative value between the various bonds issued by the same company. For instance, most companies issue senior bonds, subordinated bonds, and convertible bonds. Senior bonds give investors first claim to a company's assets should it go out of business. Convertible bonds can be converted into a fixed number of ordinary shares in the same company at a set price. Subordinated bondholders are the last of all bondholders to have a claim on the issuing company's assets if it goes out of business. The objective is to leverage the relative value between all of those different types of bonds to make a profit. There are many types of credit strategies that we can make money in, but this is a good example.

The most important feature of this alternative strategy is its correlation (or lack thereof) with all the substrategies that we outlined above. The substrategies have very little correlation between themselves. For example, the commodities strategy generally doesn't perform in the same manner as the merger arbitrage strategy, and credit usually doesn't perform in the same manner as either of the other two. These uncorrelated investments are quite beneficial to the overall performance of one's portfolio, because they keep one's investments diversified and are able to mitigate market fluctuations.

Figure 5.2: Core versus Alternative Strategies

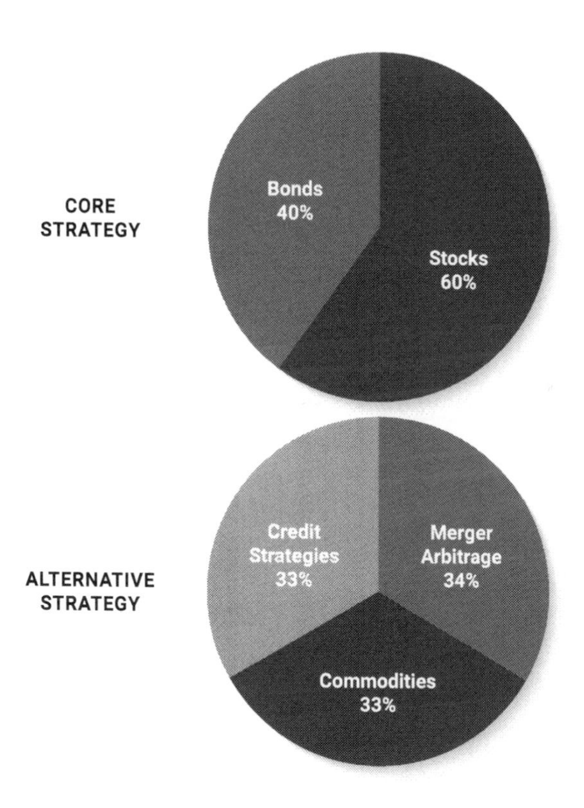

TACTICAL STRATEGY

The final strategy I want to explore is a tactical strategy. Tactical strategies generally don't have a fixed allocation to a specific asset class. Tactical strategies seek to identify areas of opportunity in which to invest when market conditions are favorable. If conditions are unfavorable, tactical strategies can have little to no exposure to risk (for example, be in cash or short-term treasuries). These strategies can reduce risk in client accounts during times of downside volatility. During large market declines, tactical strategies can theoretically sit in cash, which then can be redeployed at lower levels once the decline is over.

Stock selection portfolio. The primary objective of the stock selection portfolio is to identify and hold low-risk opportunities in the equity markets. The securities can include small-cap, medium-cap, and large-cap companies (*cap* refers to *capitalization*, or how much each company is worth, which is calculated by multiplying the number of outstanding shares by the share price). When we are fully invested, the stock selection portfolio will hold approximately fifteen positions in equities selected on the basis of fundamental and technical analyses. *Fundamental analysis* is a method of evaluating a security by examining factors such as revenue, earnings, profit margins, and cash flow. The objective of a fundamental analysis is to determine if a company is a well-run business.

I briefly mentioned *technical analysis* when I described my investment philosophy as a chartist. Essentially, a chartist is a type of technical analyst. Technical analysts uncover investment opportunities by analyzing chart patterns, historical prices, and other technical indicators. In my practice, I use both types of analyses to uncover attractive investment opportunities for my clients.

As I mentioned, the primary objective of the stock selection portfolio is to hold low-risk opportunities in the equity markets—that is, those opportunities where the potential reward in investing in the stock is expected to far outweigh the risks. One of the best ways to reduce risk in this portfolio is to maintain a strict sell discipline, which is defined in the next paragraph. An effective sell discipline will have well-defined and well-adhered-to triggers. I use a trend-following approach as part of my sell discipline, the main benefit of which is that it keeps me and my clients safely on the sidelines when the stock market is experiencing a sharp decline.

The stock selection portfolio I employ uses a simple moving

average—the average price of a stock over a specified period—to determine the trend of each stock held in the portfolio. For example, if the stock is trading above its moving average, the trend is bullish. If the stock drops below its moving average, the trend has turned bearish. Stocks remain in the portfolio as long as the trend is bullish.

Of course, this strategy is not perfect. However, it is extremely helpful in protecting investment dollars when the stock market suffers an extended decline. Very often, the best place to be during a dip in the market is waiting safely on the sidelines until the next opportunity develops.

Such a dip occurred, in fact, while I was writing this book. In particular, early in October 2018, this strategy helped Centric weather several dramatic market dips. It moved holdings to cash—30 percent on Monday and 70 percent on Wednesday, before the big market dips late in the week—not because I made a good judgment call but because the strategies that were built over the past ten years picked up on red flags in the market and responded. Automating the decision to sell further ensures that emotion is not a factor in deciding to temporarily step back from the market.

As a result, Centric's clients have experienced far less volatility than the market has. This is why strategy allocation (investing across strategies, which mitigates around ups and downs) is so much more powerful than asset allocation (holding on to your mix of stocks and bonds), smoothing out the ride for people so they don't give up on the pursuit. With a smoother ride, people are less likely to give up before they meet their goals, whatever they might be!

From an emotional standpoint, some investors have a very difficult time managing their investments during periods of extreme stock market volatility. They almost invariably make poor decisions when the market is falling. In fact, it's not uncommon for investors to liquidate their entire investment portfolio when the stock market has reached its selling climax. It's simply human nature for investors to cash out at the worst possible time, as they reach their maximum level of pain and discomfort.

It's not uncommon for investors to liquidate their entire investment portfolio when the stock market has reached its selling climax. It's simply human nature for investors to cash out at the worst possible time, as they reach their maximum level of pain and discomfort.

This is the reason why I always use a sell discipline in the stock selection portfolios we manage. It completely removes the emotion from investing, thereby preventing me and my clients from making poor investment decisions based on a hunch or a feeling or even utter panic. To generate long-term successful results, it's critically important to have a well-defined, specific plan of action. The stock selection portfolio certainly accomplishes this important objective when you set rules for the portfolio and stick to them.

Relative strength. The relative strength portfolio is designed to capture investment opportunities with low-cost ETFs. This momentum-based strategy involves identifying top-performing ETFs (essentially, mutual funds whose shares are traded like stocks) within the coverage universe, or the indexes we have chosen to create a bordered world marketplace. Very similar to the stock selection portfolio, the relative strength portfolio uses a strict sell discipline as a means of reducing risk during periods of extreme volatility.

SAYING "NO" TO EXCESSIVE FEES

Now that you've had an opportunity to review the core, alternative, and tactical strategies along with my overall investment philosophy, let's discuss two final topics that cause many investors to experience inferior performance results. These topics are paying excessive fees and allowing your emotions to control your investment decisions. Let's begin with excessive fees.

Excessive fees can be one of the largest factors in the underperformance of any investor's portfolio. It is important to understand the myriad fees charged to manage your portfolio or wealth. High fees are a good reason to move on from your current advisor. Don't get me wrong: advisors obviously need to be paid for their services. While it can be counterproductive to bargain shop when looking for a financial advisor, since you often get what you pay for, there is also a limit to how much you should be paying in fees.

An advisor should be able to tell someone exactly what they are paying, how often, and to whom. There are many potential layers of fees you can be charged for portfolio management and planning services: management fees to your advisor, expenses paid to the fund companies you may use in your portfolio, load fees assessed against your account for access to certain mutual funds, and so on. If your advisor is reluctant to give you a full accounting of all the fees you're paying, it's a good sign you're paying too much.

Another concern or red flag would be if an advisor was constantly trying to get you in a private deal or private placement. The fees are big for such instruments, and usually that is why an advisor would choose to sell them to clients. Fees are often buried in fine print, and clients have no idea what they are paying. Think of it this way: every dollar paid in fees is another dollar your portfolio needs to earn to make money for you. It's like getting hooked on a hurdle and having to drag it with you for the rest of the race—it's harder to cross the finish line when you're weighted down by an unnecessary burden.

Table 5.1: Keeping Tabs on Fees

The Fees You Should Ask About	The Range of Fees	My Recommendation	What Not to Do	Other Comments
Advisory Costs / Management Fee	Less than 1.0% to more than 2.0%	I believe 1.0% is fair.	Haggle with the advisor so much that it sours the relationship.	Paying more than 1.5% is generally considered excessive.
Expense Ratios on Any Funds Used	Ranging from near 0.1% to 2.0% per year	Your dollar weighted expense ratio shouldn't be more than 1.0%	Believe that all low cost funds are good and high cost funds are bad. It's all about how they fit into your strategy.	The average mutual fund has an expense ratio of 1.15%
Load Fees	As high as 5.75%	Many financial professionals, including myself, consider load fees unfair to the client.	If you have over $100,000 of liquid assets, don't pay loads.	Mutual funds were a great innovation but are no longer appropriate for some investors and some strategies.
Trading Costs	Between $4 and $20 for a typical trade	As long as the advisor is somewhere in the range, move on to the next discussion point.	Let this be a sticking point. Your comfort and confidence isn't worth a few bucks.	Online trading has lowered trade costs, but they can still be significant. Note: advisors do not receive any of these fees.
** EXTRA CREDIT: Try to find these for your qualified plan like a 401(k), 403(b) or 457. You'll have to find all of the above, along with plan administration fees for items such as record keeping. Administrative and record keeping costs typically range from 0.0% to 1.0%. Most participants are unaware. Add it all up and see where you land.				

Note. This table is meant to be used as a guide for those who pay their advisors a fee based on assets under management. For those who pay a flat fee to their advisor or a percentage of their net worth, the "Trading Costs" in this table may be helpful as advisors do not typically cover those.

What I find most frustrating on behalf of consumers is that the majority (I'd estimate in the range of 80 to 90 percent) of fees today are taken out of a portfolio's performance, such that consumers have no idea how much they are actually being charged, other than their advisory fee. I encourage you to work with your advisor to get crystal clear on the fees you are being charged, as transparency helps you make good decisions and play at the level of the atlas client.

Whether you pay a commission on your investments, a flat fee for your advisor's services, or a percentage of your net worth, I believe people should ultimately pay for services in the way that they are most comfortable.

THE EMOTIONAL ASPECT OF INVESTING

Finally, let's discuss how your emotions can negatively affect performance results. As I mentioned previously, most investors have a very difficult time managing themselves during periods of extreme stock market volatility. They almost invariably make poor decisions when the market is falling. This universal problem affects investors across the board, from beginners to seasoned professionals. Let's review a few of the reasons why our emotions can make us our own worst enemy when it comes to investing.

Try to remember a time when you made an investment decision that you later regretted. Specifically, what caused you to make this regrettable decision? Most likely, the decision was based on either a lack of knowledge or an emotional reaction (or, very likely, both!). These two driving forces generally cause investors the most angst.

Typically, investors are at their most vulnerable when the markets are displaying excessive volatility. Emotions such as panic, fear, and depression usually begin to surface, and if they aren't kept in check, they can compel investors to do unwise things. The best way to prevent your emotions from instigating poor investment decisions is to take control of the situation. Instead of hitting the panic button during the next stock market decline, take a deep breath and think about your long-term investment goals. Most likely, your investment goals do not include liquidating your entire portfolio in the middle of a brutal stock market plunge. Therefore, avoid the temptation to veer from your strategy; instead, concentrate on your long-term plan. Allow your strategy to dictate when you start to shift monies into cash. Emotional panic is, by definition, focusing on your feelings. Feelings make terrible investment advisors. A disciplined sell approach leaves the decision on when to sell in the hands of the strategy and should give you peace of mind.

Undoubtedly, most investors have heard the golden rule of investing: Buy low and sell high. Of course, the golden rule is a great idea in theory. However, it's much more difficult to follow this advice in the real world. Why? Because it's quite challenging to keep emotions in check as the stock market rises and falls.

A rising stock market tends to be exhilarating and euphoric, leading many investors to feel overconfident. As the stock market continues to rise, so does the euphoria. Quite often, this leads to overconfidence, which usually causes investors to place additional funds in the stock market at the worst possible time.

A declining stock market creates a completely new set of emotions. Investors experience nervousness, desperation, panic, and utter defeat. As the stock market continues to fall, the pain reaches unbearable levels, and some investors lock in their losses by selling everything when the stock market hits bottom.

This vicious cycle continues time and again as investors allow their emotions to rule their trading decisions. This explains why, in real life, most investors buy high and sell low. Fortunately, there is a fairly simple way to solve the problem of emotion as it relates to investing.

One common element can be found in all successful investors. What separates the winners from the losers in the world of investments is that successful investors have a specific plan of action. They follow this plan on a daily basis, year after year. Consistency is key.

As an investment advisor, I'm responsible for helping my clients develop an investment strategy tailored specifically to their individual goals and objectives. Providing my clients with the discipline necessary to follow the strategy we have developed is a very important part of my job.

Developing and implementing an investment strategy is the easy part. The difficult part is maintaining the strategy during both the good times and the bad times. Anybody can follow a strategy when the stock market is moving in their favor. However, when the stock market begins to drop and volatility increases, emotions can cause people to lose sight of their investment strategy. It's times like these when an investment advisor can help you stay the course.

Developing bulletproof investment strategies designed to produce long-term sustainable results while reducing the volatility that is inherently embedded in all financial markets is no small feat. For me, this process has taken many late nights, and years upon years of thought and energy. Financial experience advisors put in this work, though, using insight from market history to keep a careful watch on patterns in the market to determine the best and most risk-advised adjustments. A financial experience advisor will stay engaged, recognizing trends and tweaking strategies when necessary. Staying nimble is a must for a financial experience advisor.

CONCLUSION: INVEST IN YOURSELF

To take personal responsibility for our financial futures, we need to invest in ourselves. You are your own best, if not only, resource for accumulating wealth. Investing in yourself means spending more time on your education, refining your own skill sets, and branching out to meet new people who might help you achieve your goals. The more educated, skilled, experienced, and connected you are, the more valuable opportunities you are going to get, which means higher salaries and more options for you down the road, both of which will help you build a stronger financial foundation.

Make more money, spend less, and invest wisely. Make a detailed budget for yourself based on your projected income and your current expenses. Set firm limits on your expenses, and keep a close eye on where most of your money goes—you might be surprised by where you waste the most money and how easy it is to plug that leak. An ancient proverb notes, "Small sacrifices can lead to significant benefits." In the world of the atlas client, the saying implies that saving money can result in excellent benefits in the long run.

Not budgeting for future expenses is problematic, but at the other end of the spectrum, extreme underspending in the present may also deprive you of basic necessities.

While developing a budget, a large number of people tend to neglect certain inevitable expenses (e.g., car repairs, a new roof, large appliance replacement), and it sets the stage for many concerns in the future. Not budgeting for future expenses is problematic, but at the other end of the spectrum, extreme underspending in the present may also deprive you of basic necessities: healthy food, safe shelter, a reliable ride to work. It's great to have a significant savings, but if you refuse to make use of your money or rejoice in what you have because spending it makes you feel discontent, disgruntled, and indecisive, you might as well not have any savings for the deprivation you are imposing on yourself.

A majority of us presuppose that life will always be a garden path and we will scarcely stumble upon any reversals in our lives. Things could be running smoothly, and you may be able to afford each luxury in your life right now, but no matter how well things are going, always have a financial plan for the upcoming years: make a budget, track your expenses, and consult a financial advisor for better judgments. Whether you are employed at a firm or working for yourself, invest in a separate rainy day savings account and leave it alone until an unexpected expense arises and you absolutely need it.

Learning how to manage your money properly is a key to securing your finances in the long run. Budgeting and planning play imperative roles in formulating a financial management formula that enables you to save money without ignoring your innate needs. Understanding personal finance and having the discipline to manage a budget and save for the future are essential factors that enable the achievement of personal life goals.

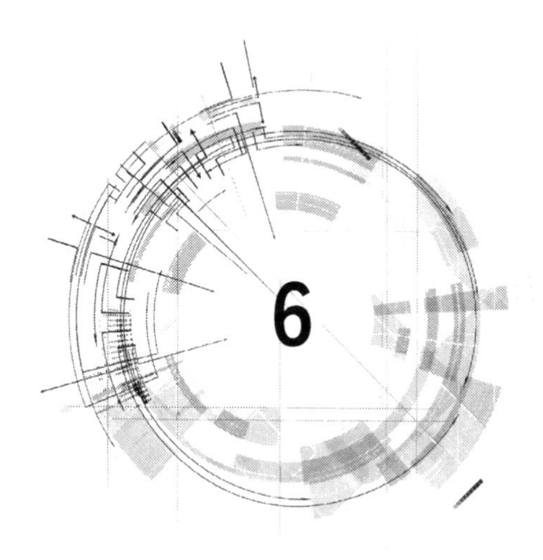

Gray Warriors: A Guide for You

If you are between the ages of ten and fifty years, the approach to money management that I just described can be quite effective. If, however, you are nearing retirement age and have less than you need to retire, like in the scenario described early in the previous chapter, you are on a short runway without much room to maneuver. Rather than throwing up your hands in hopeless desperation, I suggest getting very creative with some wealth planning ideas. Here are a few.

REVERSE MORTGAGES

Reverse mortgages are heavily marketed to older homeowners who can obtain them starting when they are sixty-two years old. Essentially, a reverse mortgage converts part of your home equity into cash. The payout, which is tied to life expectancy, can be taken as a lump sum, as a line of credit, or in monthly amounts that last as long as you or your spouse lives in the house. However, reverse mortgages are complex and laden with fees, and they don't allow you to tap all of your equity. Plus, the interest rate can be 1 to 1.5 percentage points higher than you would get by refinancing. Yes, taking on housing debt in retirement is not ideal, but for many it is unavoidable, and at least it lets you minimize your monthly payments while pulling out cash. If you believe this might be right for your situation, don't make this decision alone. Find a trusted advisor or two. They'll help you weigh the pros and cons.

CUTTING DOWN ON EXPENSES

It is time to take an honest look at where your money is currently going. That means considering not only the small things (Do you need the number of premium cable channels you pay for? Can you eat out a little less?) but the larger ones too (Do you need that second car now that your kids are out of the house?). Another example: Maybe you first bought life insurance when you had a baby. Now the baby is in law school. If your obligations are behind you—for example, your spouse could live on the money in the retirement accounts plus Social Security if you died, and the kids are on their own—then consider dropping it.

One way to dramatically lower your living expenses: move somewhere cheaper. This does not have to mean moving across the country. Trading a high-tax school district for one nearby with lower taxes can make a substantial difference. If you are willing to go a few hours—say from San Francisco, where the median home price is $685,000, to Carson City, Nevada, where it is $140,000—you can transform your standard of living. Some more adventurous souls have chosen to retire in countries in Central and South America or New Zealand, where the dollar goes much further, and have had lush and pleasurable experiences. This is a powerfully positive thing that someone can do to improve his or her retirement situation.

THE COMFORT ZONE THAT ISN'T THAT COMFORTABLE

Retirement is a modern concept with origins in military history. Until the late 1800s, those who had to work to earn their living worked their entire lives. Historians credit the Roman Empire with originating the idea of an income that continued after work service: they offered pensions to retiring soldiers during the first century BCE. While this started a long tradition of military pensions, the concept of ceasing to work in late life did not begin to spread to the rest of the workforce until the twentieth century. By 1926, larger employers in the United States had established approximately two hundred private pension systems. The pensions of these early systems were designed to pay out a low percentage of the employee's salary at retirement and were not intended to replace the employee's full final income.

The idea that employees should have a defined benefit in

retirement gained traction during the boom decades that followed World War II. Large corporate employers took a paternalistic approach to their workers and offered pensions as part of their talent recruitment and retention efforts. This was definitely a smart move, because it worked: during that time, it became common for workers to spend their entire careers at the same company. By 1970, about half of all workers were covered by pensions, and that proportion held until about 1990.

The 1970s brought staggering inflation to America. One of the many responses to this economic stressor was legislation that changed retirement forever. Congress passed The Revenue Act of 1978; its section 401(k) cleared the way for the establishment of defined contribution plans. The idea was revolutionary. It was also intended to be a tax dodge on deferred income for Kodak executives. In 1980, a benefits consultant saw the provision as a way for employers to enable employees to contribute their own money, in a tax-advantaged way, to an account that would supplement any retirement benefits the employer provided.[1]

With the rise of the 401(k), though, came the realization of businesses that maybe they didn't have to keep their employees on the payroll forever via pensions. Over time, more and more companies established 401(k)s and offered matching contributions while pulling back on pensions. Over the past thirty-eight years, for the typical US employee, the responsibility for developing a sustainable retirement income has shifted from the employer to the individual.

Saving for retirement was not always confusing. It is confusing now because the investment and tax landscape can no longer be navigated without a professional. Many try; few succeed. So much information is out there that people don't know whom to believe and trust. It has not always been this way, partially because people used to be blissfully unaware. Lack of access to information makes markets more opaque and people more willing to just accept the status quo. Another source of confusion is that people still believe the government will be there to bail them out when they run out of money in old age. That has become one of the biggest delusions of the modern age. It is time to move past this way of thinking and take personal responsibility for our financial futures.

SAVINGS

By the age of sixty years, you should have saved about seven times your current income. This assumes you will grow your portfolio by 5.5 percent annually, retire at 67, live to 92, and replace 85 percent of your preretirement income with income from Social Security and investments when you stop working. This also assumes life is drawn with straight lines and a permanent marker. If you do not have this much in savings, you may have to find part-time work, take on gig work such as consulting, or continue working full time. Whereas some older adults in this position end up feeling strained and depressed over remaining in the workforce during what are seen as the retirement years, others have been able to view this need to still earn a paycheck as an opportunity to stay vital, pursue something new, and remain socially connected. Retirement might even be considered overrated.

ANNUITY

The financial industry has long touted the "4 percent rule," which states that your retirement money should last thirty years as long as you withdraw no more than 4 percent annually. Yet life rarely goes to plan, such as in the case of unexpected medical expenses. One alternative: Convert 20 to 25 percent of your assets into an immediate income annuity that will provide a fixed income stream for the rest of your life. Seventy is a great age for this move. The older you are, the shorter your life expectancy (according to the actuarial charts—I know you're going to buck the trend!), the higher your payout.

An annuity is essentially insurance, not an investment: It will not increase in value with inflation, and when you die, the principal is gone. However, an immediate income annuity ensures you do not outlive your money. Because today's low interest rates are currently not working in your favor, it makes sense to build an annuity ladder and annuitize in chunks as you age. That is, buy small immediate annuities over a period of years, rather than jumping all-in with your first purchase, to provide guaranteed income while minimizing the risk of being locked in at a low interest rate forever. Another benefit of buying annuities in stages is that it allows you to buy them from different insurance companies, which protects you in case one of the insurance companies experiences financial trouble and suddenly is not there

One alternative: Convert 20 to 25 percent of your assets into an immediate income annuity that will provide a fixed income stream for the rest of your life.

for you. Then you invest the remainder of your nest egg to provide the growth you need to keep up with inflation.

A nest egg untouched can continue to grow, often tax free, at least until you reach the age of seventy years, when mandatory withdrawals begin. Staying employed also allows you to put off taking Social Security benefits until you reach age seventy, which brings with it an 8 percent bump in benefits for every year past your full retirement age that you delay taking them.

INSURE SMART

If you are mulling over long-term care insurance, know that you will pay for your delay: The younger you are when you apply for coverage, the lower your premiums. According to the American Association for Long-Term Care Insurance,[2] a sixty-year-old couple could get a policy for about $145 a month each. The initial benefit of $164,000 grows to $386,500 for each when the older person reaches the age of eighty-five years. If they are sixty-five years old when they purchase the insurance, that same policy will cost about $195 a month per person, and the value of the benefits when the older person reaches the age of 85 is $333,000 each. Such coverage can work for people worth more than $500,000, as their nest egg is too big to quickly spend down to qualify for Medicaid but less than the $3 million it would take to fund their continuing care.

Do you have great genes and fear outliving your savings? Longevity insurance is a less expensive policy that won't pay off unless you live to the ripe old age of eighty-five years. At that point, you will start receiving monthly sums to help with your living expenses. Say at age sixty, you buy a $50,000 policy from a major carrier. If you live to the age of eighty-five years, you will start receiving annual payouts of $15,862 if you are a man, $15,511 if you are a woman.

Don't forget about inflation! If that $50,000 policy were purchased today, twenty-five years from now, this payout money would only be worth $7,576 for a man and $7,408 for a woman in today's dollars. Some companies offer longevity insurance that has inflation protection. It is worth paying for.

SEVEN KEY CHARACTERISTICS OF A GOOD ADVISOR–CLIENT RELATIONSHIP

Most people are unaware of the number of services their financial advisors could provide for them. After all, you tend to only see them for the reason you went to them in the first place. Thus, you miss out on learning about their additional abilities that can serve you as well!

If you want to know what services your advisor offers, you must set up a service capabilities overview meeting with them. Lay out certain benchmarks to indicate when the service you are requesting must be used, like starting a 529 when you have a child or refinancing your home when interest rates drop. This meeting is also an opportunity for the advisor to bring up services they have available that you didn't realize that they had or you needed.

In the midst of all the business, though, you will maximize the effectiveness of your relationship with your financial advisor if you learn who your advisor is personally. When advisors and clients learn about one another, it establishes a level of trust that makes it easier for you to heed your advisor's warnings or advice and for your advisor to raise issues with you in the first place.

The media tends to sensationalize stories that revolve around money, which is another reason why establishing a respectful and personal bond with your advisor is so important: you want a reputable source of information who can wade through the drama and tell you what's right and what's wrong. The right advisor will make sure to connect with you on a one-on-one basis. What are characteristics of good advisors?

- **They don't rush.** They'll explain things slowly and will answer all your questions.
- **They engage feelings.** Conversations should be steered toward feelings; expect check-ins such as "How do you feel about this?"
- **They don't mind getting personal.** They show interest in your kids and your pets.
- **They are willing to have a social lunch.** Go out to lunch but talk no shop.
- **They stay in touch via social media.** Social media sites like Facebook, Twitter, and LinkedIn allow people to share key life events such as weddings, births, job changes, and so on.
- **They listen when you talk about your own family.**

Share details about your own family; your advisor may have some ideas about how to structure your financial life to provide for and protect them.

- **You feel comfortable opening your home to them.** Invite your financial advisor to your home. You may well find yourself also invited to theirs.

All of these aspects combined enable an effective bond to be forged between the financial advisor and the client.

CONCLUSION: IT MATTERS NOT HOW STRAIT THE GATE

It is often said that anyone can steer a ship in calm waters, but it takes competence at the helm to navigate treacherous seas like the ones we sometimes find ourselves in. Health care costs are rising, the federal debt is increasing, inflation is threatening, and my perception is that very few people are competent to effectively navigate the crippling times we may encounter. During what we once considered the calmer waters of the past, growth (or at least the illusion of it) was literally taken for granted. But look what has happened since the economic storms moved in: there appears to be more reactive behavior than proactive, innovative action. This is why financial experience advisors are needed. They will lead those of advanced ages through the troubled waters to the smooth sailing of the golden years just beyond the horizon.

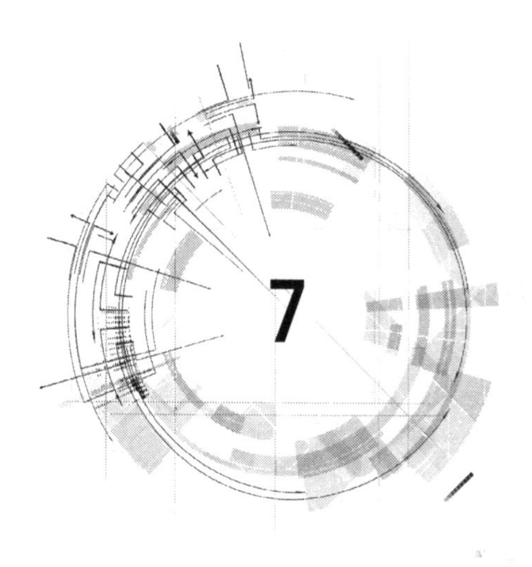

Digital Dawn: Navigating the Future

There is much debate in the public space about the concept of *singularity*, the hypothetical moment when software becomes self-aware. Think about that for a moment: tech will become as self-aware as we are, in effect, creating sentient artificial intelligence (AI). Can technology really take a fundamentally human characteristic and adopt it for its own purposes? Is it time to make a tinfoil hat and consider whether world domination has been technology's nefarious goal all along? In all seriousness, high-profile thinkers like Elon Musk and Bill Gates argue that singularity may be closer than we think.

In fact, the year 2047 gets a lot of attention in their writings. Musk has gone on the record as saying AI is more dangerous than nuclear weapons. Gates has echoed these warnings and asked why everyone isn't more concerned. When leading tech visionaries worry about the effect of technological advances on humankind, is it any wonder that the rest of us occasionally worry about the pace of technological change and what effect it is going to have on our daily lives?

It is important to note that the pace of technological change is exponential, not linear. One hundred years ago, electricity was still a novelty. In the 1950s, computers were an expensive and cumbersome investment, the provenance of governments, universities, and large corporations. A five-megabyte drive weighed two thousand pounds and required a forklift to transport. A mere six decades later, the smallest iPhone 8 has a sixty-four gigabyte drive and weighs a mere 5.2 ounces. The future is closing in on us much faster than we think it is.

In the past decade alone, new technologies have affected everything from how we connect with friends, to how we get around, to how we manage our money; think FaceTime, Uber, and Apple Wallet. This kind of disruption happens in the face of considerable uncertainty, something I refer to as *friction*, or the hurdles that any new tech faces in being adopted by the consumer. Friction explains why Uber succeeds and Google Glass fails. Uber consumers overcame the friction of getting into the car with a stranger because drivers had consumer ratings to keep them in check—and weren't traditional taxi drivers also strangers anyway? Google Glass did not take off because as useful and cool as a personal heads-up display was, frankly, people did not want to walk down the street wearing such a contraption on their head. The product never had a chance.

Friction explains why Uber succeeds and Google Glass fails.

The friction factor is particularly interesting when we consider the financial industry, where people tend to feel safest with the traditional way of doing things. When it comes to money, people often like tried and true. Yet online banking hasn't killed the bank teller. In the Specialization Age, successful *fintech* companies (which specialize in developing technology for the financial services industry) are going to anticipate where the friction is likely to be and work around it. Venmo hit that sweet spot, with $17.6 billion spent on it in 2016,[1] and companies like Zelle are popping up as competition. Are we in a race to the finish line to see which person-to-person payment system prevails, or is each here to stay in the Specialization Age, where different consumers have different wants and needs and thus the market can support multiple systems? A consumer survey shows that those who like Zelle appreciate it for its privacy, whereas those who prefer Venmo enjoy its social aspect.[2]

The uncertainty and pace of change, taken together, force us to ponder some uncomfortable questions that arise where technology and finances collide. Will robo-advisors eliminate the need for human involvement in investing? Can the new fintech really help investors? In this chapter, I address these disruptions and discuss what I believe will be their most significant outcomes.

THE RISE OF THE ROBO-ADVISORS

Many people's idea of an advisor is a midcareer male professional in a suit, sitting in his office and selling investments for a living. Honestly, in today's world, that picture is not that far off from the reality. However, what a financial advisor of the future looks like may be completely different. Is it possible that your kids' idea of a financial advisor will be an app on a smart phone? Are we ready to ask Siri for money advice? How much friction will the financial industry endure and absorb as fintech evolves? How will they do in a bear market? Already we are seeing the success of robo-advisors, automated investment services that use algorithms to give out formulaic investment advice that is based on information input by the client. Robo-advisors, also known as *e-advisors* or *digital advisors*, have captured the attention of those who are seeking financial services, in no small part because of the low fees charged for using them.

Already we are seeing the success of robo-advisors, automated investment services that use algorithms to give out formulaic investment advice that is based on information input by the client.

How did the success of the robo-advisor come about? In 2008, the financial services industry was not addressing the needs of people who did not fit a specific mold: if you were a mid- to late-career professional with over $200,000 available to invest, there was a financial advisor eager to take you on as a client. Younger, less wealthy people need not apply. The creators of the first robo-advisors stepped in to fill the service gap. With fees a fraction of what traditional advisors would charge and no account minimums, automated tools made investing accessible to anyone over the age of 18 years. This low-fee, easy-access approach explains the early success of platforms like Wealthfront and Betterment (both available online and as iOS or Android apps), which combine investment strategies with software so that you don't have to worry about the nuances of creating or rebalancing a portfolio. A viable alternative to the suit-and-tie advisor was born.

Traditional advisors expected that the robos would appeal to the tech-savvy millennial generation. They did not think robo-advisors would shift the industry much, because millennials, with their modest account balances, weren't ideal clients, anyway. That attitude changed when older and more affluent investors began to flock to the automated platforms. That is, the shift in investor preferences paralleled the uses of technology in all other areas of the broader economy.

Why did this happen? I can see two reasons. The first one is something I refer to as "the grandma effect." When millennials went away to college, social media boomed with the promise of an easy way to connect and stay in touch with friends (as well as share cat pictures, photos of feet on the beach, and the not as yucky but still weird food pictures, of course). Everyone expected the younger generation to jump on the social media bandwagon, so there was no big surprise there, but baby boomers and Gen Xers followed in the millennials' wake, mostly in an effort to stay in the conversation with their kids and grandkids. Once baby boomers and Gen Xers became used to the technology, the obvious next step was to explore service-providing online channels, like the robos. The second reason is the core proposition of the robos: low-cost portfolio management is a valuable service for investors of any age, and lower fees can make a difference in how long retirement savings can last.

ARE YOU READY FOR A GOOGLE FINANCIAL ADVISOR?

The early success of purely automated advice platforms was impressive: $19 billion under management by 2014, a mere four years after the first robo-advisors made their entrance. The business model has proven to be so promising that household names like Vanguard and Charles Schwab have launched similar services. However, growth rates have since slowed down for two big reasons.

First, the extremely low fees that served as a key selling point for early adaptors proved to be unsustainable. The costs of acquiring new clients are high, and economies of scale aren't sufficient to offset those costs.

Second and more important, automated platforms are far from being advisors. In fact, a more appropriate name would be *automated rebalancing engines*. Sure, robos may be great at monitoring the market, executing trade algorithms, and performing tax-loss harvesting (the practice of selling a security that has experienced a loss and, by realizing the loss, offsetting taxes on both gains and income; the sold security is then replaced with a similar one). However, they cannot absorb the entirety of an individual's financial situation, including student loans, mortgages, aging parents, and plans to start a family. It seems an app has yet to be written that can account for every potential variable of the human financial condition.

Financial experience advisors can close the gap left by the robo-advisors by offering an affordable subscription-based service designed for individuals making, say, at least $60,000 a year or for those with less than $200,000 to invest. Think of it as Netflix for financial advising. For something like $299 a month, consumers could chat, call, Skype, or meet in person with their advisor four times a year, plus have access to the proprietary tech of the advisory firm. This is just one fee-for-financial-advice model that could work. The result could be a marriage of humans and tech that is affordable, useful, and scalable.

PROS AND CONS OF USING A ROBO-ADVISOR

Pros

- They have powerful investment algorithms that work as long as you use the narrow and specific portfolio they are offering.

- They require a low minimum balance (which helps the little guy).
- You can marry them with a financial advisor: you have to pay a bit more, but some robos offer a human financial advisory contact that you can call for planning purposes.
- They offer the ability to go with "gut answers" on their Risk Tolerance Questionnaires, which may help those that tend to overthink everything.
- It is easy to "set-it-and-forget-it," which might help mitigate panic selling or other behavioral biases.

Cons

- You are paying into a broad-based asset allocation portfolio that may not meet your specific goals.
- They are portrayed as being extremely cheap, but the fees are actually comparable to what asset managers are charging for money management.
- They do not provide personalized service or a brick-and-mortar office to visit.
- The Risk Tolerance Questionnaires aren't as detailed as a risk assessment process that can be provided by an experienced advisor.
- Investors with low confidence and low understanding may panic and sell as the market dips without a human to walk them away from the ledge.

ROBO LEGACY: TAKING INVESTMENT ADVICE TO THE NEXT LEVEL

Despite the slowdown in their rate of growth, robo-advisors do not seem to be in immediate danger of disappearing into obscurity. In fact, popular features pioneered by robo platforms, such as a responsive client dashboard and a secure document vault, are being incorporated into the technology offerings provided by financial advisors. What's more, the way in which robo-advisors have made information accessible to the average person is leading to a renaissance of investment advice. Having experienced the convenience of getting customized investment updates 24/7, investors are pushing for the same from their human advisors, revitalizing the industry while demanding new levels of service.

The upgrades to the traditional experience do not stop with on-demand access. Providing everything from intuitive and beautiful client portals to paperless account opening, advisors are incorporating the best innovations to give their clients a perfect blend of technology and the human touch. Cloud technology has allowed advisors to offer secure online document vaults, so a client can walk around with a full library of key financial documents in his or her pocket. Account aggregation—pulling together account information from different systems and even different custodial companies—gives advisors a look at a given client's full financial picture of assets and liabilities, which can better inform their financial guidance. For investors, those improvements give access to a level of advice, customization, and timeliness that was once reserved for high-net-worth families. Today's financial advisors have advanced way beyond giving only investment advice, which is mission creep that a broker from the 1980s couldn't even have wrapped his head around.

TECHNOLOGY EMPOWERS ADVISORS TO DELIVER FINANCIAL ADVICE DIFFERENTLY

In addition to powering a highly accessible on-demand service model through self-service client portals and mobile apps, new technology has created a renewed focus on goals-based planning. Most advisors will tell you that when it comes to investing, the true risk is not the market (this will be true until the market declines by 60% or more). In reality, many investors fail to achieve personal financial goals because of bad habits and poor decision-making. Goals-based financial planning places the client's interests, goals, and fears at the center of the wealth-building puzzle. After all, if you can see the whole picture, it's easier to keep working toward the goal.

Technology can allow clients to make progress and stay on track. For example, the best client-facing applications and portals help investors automate good habits and remove emotion from decisions. To accomplish that, the new technologies apply gamification concepts (i.e., methods of applying game-playing, point-scoring, and competition to other areas of activity, typically as an online marketing technique to encourage engagement with a product or service) that make goals tangible and demonstrate long-term consequences of decisions that could potentially stall or sabotage progress. For example, you can very easily model a $10,000 distribution from your IRA in which you would have to pay taxes on and forgo the growth that would have been made on that money. The mobile and real-time nature of apps also allows the advisor to stay connected to the client, monitor account changes, and offer just-in-time advice on a scale that was previously impossible.

THE ISSUES OF EQUALITY IN THE TECH ERA

The industrial economies and corporations of the last two centuries have put an enormous emphasis on equality of opportunity as a central value. For example, all the misguided attempts at installing socialism around the world were based on this value. This new era, which is based on tech, will, in many ways, emphasize just the opposite. Because technological innovation always disrupts existing relationships and structures, it also introduces greater amounts of inequality to access to opportunity. However, this represents a creative difference; that is, it is not based on having more of what already exists but rather on creating entirely new kinds of opportunities, capabilities, and value. Creative inequality is not based on having a bigger piece of the existing pie but rather on using the real pie in a way that maximizes it and on continually making many more pies, all of them larger than what now exists. The fundamental structure of the world is fractal and tends to replicate itself. Pie all around!

CONCLUSION: ROBOS AND HUMANS—BETTER TOGETHER

Pure robo-advisors cannot be the future of financial advice, primarily because they offer a limited number of investment models and don't allow for human complexity. Automated investment platforms are a great fit for someone whose financial and life situations are simple. However, even those with a straightforward set of needs may find themselves wishing for the human touch when the market inevitably hits a bump or when their life circumstances change.

Luckily, today's investors aren't limited to a black-and-white choice between automated advice and traditional investment firms. In the battle between the two, hybrid models of human advice powered by technology are emerging as the ultimate winner. As technology is becoming capable of complex market monitoring, the advisor's role is shifting away from picking stocks and toward serving as a financial coach and educator—a role that you should now recognize as that of the financial experience advisor. Again, we are way beyond money management. Investment management never has been and never will be true wealth management. This is due in large part to the fact that people and their financial lives are far more than the investments they make.

The standard of what's expected from a financial advisor has been raised. Advisors now must educate clients on the nature of investment risk, decision-making biases, and the basics of investment theory. Financial advisors who personalize the wealth-building experience must shift the conversation from "What did the market do this quarter?" toward the client's goals, dreams, lifestyle, and legacy. If you think this is a much bigger conversation, you are absolutely right! This is one of the reasons why I have proposed that the title of *financial advisor* should evolve, just as the job has.

The other shift happening in the industry is a move away from merely managing the wealth already accumulated in the client's account to helping him or her accumulate wealth in the first place. Most people know that to accumulate wealth, they must earn more, save more, spend less, and invest their savings wisely. Knowing those things is the easy part; actually doing them is tough.

Most money problems don't exist because of market performance.

People have financial challenges because they are human and they make mistakes. Our brains are wired to prioritize today's wants over long-term needs. That's why the most sophisticated investment model is worthless if a client cannot execute it in a disciplined way. My experiences have taught me that the biggest value of financial advice is in helping clients stick to the plan. The tough part in creating long-term financial security isn't about managing investment strategies—it's about managing human nature.

Oddly enough, this is a problem that computers can help solve. The challenge with spur-of-the-moment decisions that can potentially derail your retirement plans is that they must be addressed when they happen, not when your account statements are finalized at the end of the quarter. Your advisor cannot be there physically to hold your hand and talk sense into you before you make a dramatic money move, but technology can. New investing tools and platforms can project the after-tax impact of your decision to sell a security when the market takes a turn for the worse. Automated check-in messages allow advisors to take the pulse of their clients' comfort levels with portfolio performance. Technology helps advisors reach clients just in time to make a difference where and when it counts.

On the quest to incorporate technology into financial services, we must walk the line between chaos and order, between new school and old school. If the tech being introduced creates too much friction, the resultant tension may bring down attempts at innovation. If we simply continue to do things the old way, upstart disruptors will emerge and transform the financial industry without our input. We must navigate the fine line between the two, adopting the new things that will provide value to clients while holding on to what already works.

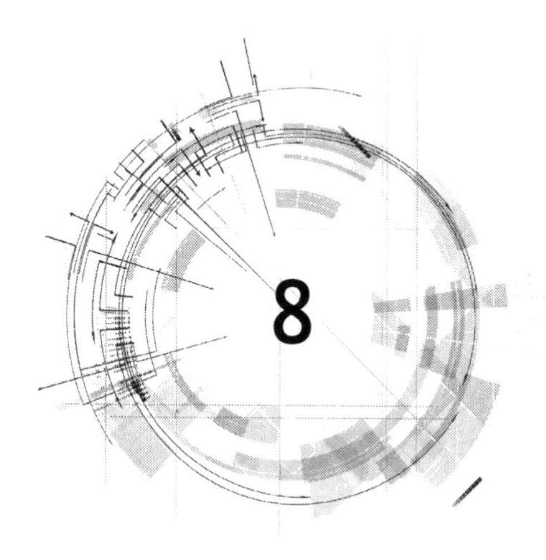

We Are All Living Longer

I plan to live to be 120 years old.

There, I said it. It may sound ambitious, but odds and science are on my side.

Let's dig into the age question for a minute, because it is a critical one. When it comes to financial planning, a good guess about your expected longevity is an important input. We want our money to outlast us. No one can predict life expectancy with 100 percent certainty, but the math requires us to make an educated guess. If you (or your financial planner) are using an outdated life expectancy statistic, you risk running out of money at an age that does not welcome money surprises.

So let's talk statistics. A child born in the United States in 1900 could expect to live, on average, to be fifty years old. Since then, advances in hygiene and medicine have dramatically lowered the rate of infant mortality (which immediately improved average life expectancy). Better drugs, treatments for chronic diseases, and positive lifestyle changes (for example, shifting away from smoking, adopting exercise routines, developing an awareness of nutritional values, and gaining better access to nutrient-dense foods) also helped humans make great strides in longevity. The positive effects did not take long to manifest themselves. In 2014, there were 44 percent more centenarians in the United States as there were in 2000, (that's about 72,000 and counting), and by 2050 the count of centenarians in the United States is projected to be as high as a million.[1] Those who do not make it to one hundred years of age still have a good chance of living into their nineties.

When it comes to financial planning, a good guess about your expected longevity is an important input. We want our money to outlast us.

Those projections are fairly modest. In the words of Art De Vany, an economist and evolutionary nutritionist, aging is not programmed; it is the result of the failure of a renewal program.[2] If we can short-circuit that failure, we can theoretically stop aging. Extending life span isn't the ultimate goal; after all, stretching out years of sickness and infirmity is not anyone's dream. As the medical field makes advances in MRI imaging, organ replacement, prosthetics, and immunotherapy, human functional life span (in other words, years of good health) can become longer. And don't forget the potential life-lengthening effects of genetic therapy, nutrition, and promising chemical compounds. It may not be possible to reverse aging, but science is making leaps toward slowing it down.

The disruptions in the medical and scientific realms mean that financial planners need to approach the common client question of "Will I outlive my money?" from a new angle. Trusted formulas no longer work, old assumptions must be challenged, and even the definition of a financial plan must be expanded.

ESTIMATES OF AVERAGE LIFE SPANS USED FOR PLANNING MUST CHANGE

A study done by *InvestmentNews*[3] found that as recently as five to ten years ago, 51 percent of advisors created retirement plans with the assumption that their clients would live to be eighty-five to ninety-four years of age, and only 27 percent planned for a life span that lasted to an age in the range of ninety-five to ninety-nine. Only 3 percent created financial plans with the assumption that their clients would break through the centennial age barrier. A woman in the United States who turned 65 in 2015 has better than a one-in-three chance of reaching her ninetieth birthday.[4] Are you financially prepared to live to eighty-five? Ninety? Ninety-five? One hundred? Or beyond? If you are like me, you don't want to take even a one-in-four chance that you will be that someone who lives to ninety but who planned to live to eighty-nine. Whoops!

Why are many of us not planning far enough into the future? Too many financial advisors are using outdated estimates for how long people will be living. Some advisors may engage in willful blindness regarding true life spans in the future; others may not have caught up with the true state of things today. It certainly doesn't help that the government only updates every ten years the mortality tables that financial advisors, the media, and the public rely on. Consumers only add to the challenge by trusting that Social Security will be there to take care of them when their own retirement funds run out, in spite of concerns that Social Security may run out of money in 2034. In 2017, the Trustees Report noted that the theoretical combined trust fund balances were expected to run out in 2034, and that's the same projection that the 2018 report made.[5]

At the time of this book's writing, my wife has a grandmother who is ninety-nine years old. I hear stories like this all the time now. Financial experience advisors and the atlas clients they serve need to collectively pull their heads out of the sand. Given the pace of improving medical technology today—researchers are on the precipice of curing cancer, HIV/AIDS, cystic fibrosis, and Alzheimer's—why don't we take these facts into account with our financial planning? As science, medicine, and technology work together to normalize the hundred-year life span, financial plans must match that expectation.

Greater longevity creates room for uncertainty. How long will clients live? How active will they remain? What costs can they expect, and what would it take to live a life that isn't just long but also healthy, active, and fulfilled? Those sound like soul-searching questions, and they highlight the need for financial planners to step away from formulas and numbers (although there is a place and a need for them during the planning process) and to assume the role of an advisor, a counselor, and a coach. That's where the financial experience advisor comes in.

FINANCIAL EXPERIENCE ADVISORS AND ATLAS CLIENTS WORK TOGETHER TO PREPARE FOR THE FUTURE

Financial experience advisors and their atlas clients plan for the modern world—for the potential for a long and healthy life that now awaits so many of us. Here is how I see the definition and scope of financial planning changing over the next decades, with financial experience advisors and atlas clients leading the way. Financial experience advisors and atlas clients will work together to

- establish a source of cash flow, saving more money for longer years of retirement;
- determine how to afford health care, putting together a plan to cover the anticipated costs of medical needs that are likely to arise with longer living; and
- engage in estate planning, establishing and evaluating the strategies and structures that will maximize the wealth and ease its transfer to the intended recipients.

Again, the engaged, holistic approach that typifies financial experience advisors and atlas clients is very important in the structure of all three of these tasks. Even more important is the relationship between these team players. Teamwork makes the dream work. With this in mind, let's take a look at the central aspects of cash flow, health care, and estate planning.

CASH FLOW AND BUDGETING ARE STILL CRITICAL

Providing for a greater number of years of life means saving more money. That, in turn, requires a strong understanding of income and expense flows: in other words, budgeting. I know that the subject of budgeting is not sexy or appealing. Most people associate budgets with scarcity and austerity. That explains why many financial planners find themselves having to sell the idea of budgeting to their clients. Resistance is not pretty. Here is what it sounds like from my end:

- "I don't need a formal budget. I can keep track of my income and expenses in my head!"

- "I make good enough money that I don't need to count every dollar."
- "I have never kept a budget, and things have always worked out fine."

Resistance exists in spite of the fact that budgeting is critical to achieving one's financial goals.

Here's the good news. While it's true that budgeting involves discipline, a common misconception is that budgeting takes away the enjoyment and pleasures of today. In fact, knowing how much money you really have and consciously managing it may make it easier for you to say no to certain things so that you can say yes to other things. For example, it's easier to resist putting that addition on your home if you know that carrying on with the space you have means you can vacation more often (within a budget, you don't have to feel guilty about enjoying yourself).

While it's true that budgeting involves discipline, a common misconception is that budgeting takes away the enjoyment and pleasures of today.

Admittedly, saying no to something today to save for retirement in the distant future can be hard. Yet, consider this: a budget isn't always about saying no to yourself; it can be about saying no to the companies that are taking more of your money than you need to give them. Once you identify these extras, you can then fix these identified problems, reducing costs by doing things like switching to a different cell phone carrier to lower your cell phone bill or dropping the bonus features of the cable service that you hardly use. As budgeting helps you save money in certain areas, it painlessly frees up more cash to put toward retirement. By putting in the legwork to create a budget up front, you can put your spending on a sort of autopilot that makes it clear when you can say yes and when you can say no, removing the hassle and guilt that can come with assessing financial decisions on a daily basis. With some creativity, you can even make saving for retirement fun by building in incentives, like taking yourself out to eat or buying a new pair of shoes every time you hit a certain milestone. Saving doesn't have to be entirely about deprivation!

In reality, a budget is just a way of aligning your money with your values, a tool for creating financial integrity. If you want to have a comfortable retirement, if you believe in giving to charity, if you want to plan for your children's future, your budget will reflect that. Your budget is not a heavy stick wielded for punishment. It does not have to be rigid or time-consuming. There are apps that make budget setup and tracking virtually effortless. Yes, clients still have to be accountable—but the mechanical aspects of keeping the budget and creating a pattern of saving money can be delegated to an algorithm.

I think one of the biggest impacts financial planners can make is in serving as an accountability mechanism and a coach for clients who struggle with getting a handle on their money matters. To me, enabling the financial experience advisor to act as an accountability mechanism starts with using a piece of technology that tracks your assets as well as all of your financial goals—essentially, it's a Fitbit for your financial life. Your financial experience advisor would have access to your data and be able to see, in real time, what kind of progress you are making toward your goals. As an atlas client, you are aware that your financial experience advisor can see what you're up to, and knowing that someone else is also following the numbers can help guide your day-to-day decision-making.

TREAT SOCIAL SECURITY AS A BONUS

Only about three or four generations of Americans have had the luxury of viewing Social Security as a main source of income in retirement. Younger people must get used to thinking about Social Security as a bonus: something that would be nice to get but does not represent the bulk of post-retirement income.

The financial outlook for the Social Security program has been uncertain for years, and academic papers criticize the program's projections as being overly optimistic and not absolutely transparent. Short of a deep reform, there are three ways to correct the Social Security funding shortfall: increase the retirement age, lower the amounts of expected payouts, or do both. No matter which path the government chooses, retirees must take charge of their own retirement savings and not count solely on Social Security.

YOU MUST PLAN FOR HEALTH CARE EXPENSES

Longer life spans likely mean more health care costs. Let's be honest: health care is expensive, and older age usually brings with it more visits to the doctor. That means average medical expenses over the course of one's retirement will likely land somewhere between high and astronomical. Your financial plan must include a projection of medical expenses because, contrary to the common misconception, Medicare won't take care of it all.

Remember that Medicare is a combination of several subplans. Most of them come with monthly premiums. Medicare Part A, which covers certain hospital expenses, is the only part of the program that does not come with a price tag. The rest of the coverages, including those for prescription drugs; dental, vision, and eye care; and any expenses not covered by the basic Medicare plan, must be purchased separately. Then you are still responsible for co-pays, coinsurance, and out-of-pocket expenses. A good projection of health care expenses in retirement should take into consideration life span, family history, personal lifestyle choices, inflation, and expectations of Medicare funding.

Long-term-care insurance (LTCI) can also be part of an effective longevity-covering financial plan. LTCI is an insurance product that helps pay for costs associated with long-term care that are not covered by health insurance, Medicare, or Medicaid. Individuals who require long-term care are generally not sick in the traditional sense but are unable to perform two of the six activities of daily living: dressing, bathing, eating, toileting, continence, and transferring (getting in and out of a bed or chair and walking). It is estimated that one in five people will need some sort of long-term care.

Tax planning can be your secret weapon in preparing for health care (and other) expenses expected to arise in old age. The problem with traditional retirement is that it's very similar to being laid off from your job: you still have your normal expenses (housing, food, clothing, and health care), but you no longer have a steady flow of new income to pay them. Your savings must last as long as possible, and smart tax planning can help. Using tax-advantaged accounts like 401(k)s, IRAs, and health savings accounts (HSAs) can help you augment the amount you save and allow it to grow tax free.

Carefully timing the withdrawals within tax-advantaged accounts, making strategic decisions about which securities to sell, and planning for tax expenses make for one complex puzzle. Even the smartest and best-educated atlas clients benefit from having a financial experience advisor by their side as they navigate these waters.

A financial experience advisor is armed with a "bucket" approach to health care costs. Different buckets are assigned to different types of medical expenses. Your two main buckets are your HSA and your ICE bucket. An HSA can be used for a myriad of basic medical expenses like co-pays, over-the-counter medications, prescriptions, and the like. Think "the things that cost less than $100 each." Your ICE bucket is "in case of emergency." You can tap into these monies for surgeries and hospital stays.

RETIREMENT LIVING ISN'T WHAT IT USED TO BE

Living longer spells a need to redefine the way people live in retirement. Retirement and assisted living facilities have evolved from the stereotypical, shudder-inducing elder warehouses of the past, where excitement meant shuffling off to play bingo once a week. Today's retirement living is both active and multigenerational. If you have thirty or forty years of retirement to look forward to, it makes sense to spend some time giving careful thought to what you want to do with that time and consulting with your financial experience advisor to get your financial house in order to ensure you can make your vision happen. In effect, retirement living is about home planning for the long term.

Yet it's more than that: It's about dreaming up the ultimate *something* worth both working toward and waiting for. Your financial experience advisor will have the experience, know-how, and connections to guide the conversation, alert you to different potential options, encourage your aspirations, and put you in touch with the people who can help you actualize the future you envision, no matter how out of reach you think it might be.

Tomorrow's retirees have many possibilities for how to structure their living situations. Some may choose age-specific communities for their social safety net, their encouragement of active living, and the possibility of being independent longer. Others look to build co-living structures to accommodate extended families and benefit from intergenerational support. Some retirees consider the ever-increasing costs of renting and opt to live on a houseboat; others look at the cost of assisted living and decide that the comparable cost of cruising full time, with the added bonus of international travel, is worth having no fixed address.[6] Options abound, and that means you get to shape your retirement living to fit your needs and preferences in a way that would have been unusual or impossible fifty years ago.

Also consider redefining the concept of retirement in a way that works for you. Although some people enjoy taking the traditional approach of leaving the workforce permanently, others prefer to take a series of sabbaticals: working, taking a break, and working again. Others choose to continue working, but in a new career field they are passionate about, while others take a part-time job with benefits like more time on the golf greens. There are multiple possibilities, well befitting the atlas client who is taking responsibility for one's life and customizing his or her retirement rather than falling into the way things have seemingly always been done.

Be sure to tap into the resources your financial experience advisor will bring to the table as you plan for your life beyond work. The effort the two of you put in now can make the golden years truly a treasure.

ESTATE PLANNING LOOKS DIFFERENT, TOO

Legacy planning takes on a whole new look as more money is needed to get aging retirees through a longer life span. Reverse mortgages and other financial tools create an immediate need for more openness in the money conversation among generations. This can be challenging for families that have historically treated money as a taboo subject.

Every family's financial situation is different. Multiply that by the complexities of interfamily relationships and you get a tough estate-planning equation to solve. No matter what complications may seem pressing, begin with the basics. If you are not having conversations about tax liability, budgeting, wills, and trusts, you are exposing your family to a high degree of financial risk. When it comes to legacy planning, the goal is no surprises.

LIFESTYLE PLANNING IS THE NAME OF THE GAME

It amazes me how many people do not have the necessary pieces in place for effective estate planning. Perhaps it is because most of us don't like to think about our mortality; perhaps it is also because we are so busy in today's world that estate planning keeps taking a backseat to those things we deem to be higher priority items. A disconcerting conversation I have with many of my new clients goes like this:

> Will: "Do you have your will in place?"
>
> Client: "No."
>
> Will: "Do you have a trust set up?"
>
> Client: "No..."
>
> Will: "Do you have durable power of attorney?"
>
> Client: "Wait... What?"
>
> Will: "You do realize the potential consequences of these answers, right? God forbid you get hit by a bus tomorrow, you are going to lose half of your estate to probate and you'll be lucky if the rest goes to your heirs in eighteen months."

People need to start confronting the reality that if they do not take responsibility for estate planning, they risk losing much of what they've worked so hard all of their lives to build, to say nothing of the complex legal and financial issues that their families will inherit at a time when they really should be able to grieve and heal from their loss.

The best advice I can give on estate planning is "do it." Get your wills and trusts done. Get a durable power of attorney. Define what you want to happen to you if you become incapacitated. The role of the financial experience advisor here is to get you connected to a trust and estates lawyer that you can get to know, like, and trust. If you currently have a lawyer, the financial experience advisor needs to be in contact with this person, and the communication must be open and free-flowing. Only then will both parties be able to set you up with a solid plan.

CONCLUSION: A LONGER FUTURE, TOGETHER

Longer life spans demand that what life looks like during the older years be reimagined. I believe that the idea of full retirement as thirty years of knitting, fishing, and sitting in a rocking chair will be phased out. More and more people are opting for a combination of semiretirement and remaining active in the community instead.

Longer life spans demand that what life looks like during the older years be reimagined.

The importance of working longer is self-evident: retaining even a portion of your income can help stretch your savings considerably because it slows down the rate of withdrawals. A longer career and active involvement in the community can have other positive side effects: they can help you live longer and remain healthier.

We all know intuitively that staying engaged and involved in projects outside of yourself makes for a happier life. The great news is that such engagement may also create conditions that extend your life. Research by National Geographic Fellow Dan Buettner, author of *The Blue Zones Solution*, has identified engagement in family and social life as two of the nine shared characteristics of people who enjoy longer and more functional life spans.[7]

Then there is research by the Stanford Center on Longevity and the idea of the *social portfolio*.[8] Their study suggests that building strong social connections can contribute to physical, financial, and emotional well-being. Working for pay and volunteering are two of the nine metrics that the study used for measuring social connectedness. I believe social portfolios should become an integral part of retirement planning—on par with the investment portfolio.

In summary, the fact that we live in an age when life is getting longer means that planning for older age must take on a new level of urgency and depth. Holistic life planning isn't just about lining up Social Security payments and 401(k) plans anymore! I predict that in the future, financial experience advisors will take on active roles as advocates and coaches for their clients on everything from budgeting to lifestyle choices in retirement.

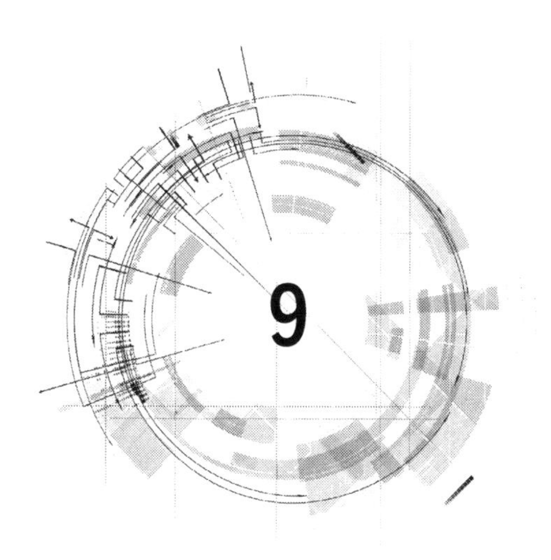

Atlas Aligned: Final Thoughts

The markets are a force of nature—by definition, a double-edged sword. Fabulous wealth has been created in financial markets; but the markets can devastate wealth as well. We cannot throw away the markets; we can only manage the issues they throw at us. We must deal with the market on its terms, not ours. The financial experience advisor and the knowledge within this book are the remedies for these problems. Since the financial experience advisor is there expressly to aid you in ways the market cannot, the overall relationship between the financial experience advisor and you is paramount. This connection is

Will you float with the current toward an unknowable destination or chart a course to your own goals, proceeding under your own steam?

the glue that keeps everything together and is the antidote to intertwined forces of nature like greed and fear. We are all at some time afflicted by these two diseases, which can take up much of our mental faculties. How do we combat that? How do we break through our natural-born habits? A financial experience advisor's primary purpose is to help pull you toward the other sides of both of those spectrums—toward faith instead of fear and toward contentment instead of greed.

The right partnership with your financial advisor determines whether you will merely experience market events as they unfold or whether you will be an atlas client who starts plotting your own course to your own goals, guided by a vision of what your life could be. As we have discussed, this new age is no longer a zero-sum game. There are no longer winners and losers per se, since everyone can be a winner. So what kind of winner do you want to be?

It boils down to a choice: in seizing your piece of the ever-expanding pie, will you float with the current toward an unknowable destination or chart a course to your own goals, proceeding under your own steam?

MAKING THE ATLAS SHIFT

The crux of my argument in this book has been that the time has come for millions of people to make the transition to financial maturity. So many of society's problems—poverty, crime, and so forth—occur because people are unable to get themselves out of economic infancy. They possess none of the tools, knowledge, or habits to take control of their financial affairs and to overcome their dependency on large organizations.

One point should be evident by now: The Specialization Age has arrived, and there is nothing that politicians, corporate executives, or lawyers can do about it. The powers that be in our world will continually put up obstacles and roadblocks, but these barriers will always be overcome by the enormous ingenuity and capability of financial experience advisors and atlas clients. The only question is whether advisors and consumers will recognize the extraordinary opportunities in front of them and take the steps necessary to enter and thrive in the Specialization Age. Never has there been a more exciting time to be an investor or a financial advisor.

GIVING BACK IN THE AGE OF SPECIALIZATION

We are tribal beings by nature. The majority of people want to do well not only for themselves but for their communities. People have this idea that they want to make a difference in the world; with impact investing, you can blur the line between making money and enacting some amount of change. The old way of giving back is to declare something like, "I'm going to join the Peace Corps," and while there is certainly value to serving the world through nonprofit organizations, this no longer is the only way to make a difference. For example, many companies worldwide are either melting down or repurposing unwanted plastic refuse and turning it into usable products or fuel—and they are making boatloads of money doing it.[1] In the Specialization Age, you can turn a profit while you are giving back and doing good. Talk about a win-win!

Wealth has always had the ability to be a force for good. Now, sustainable, responsible, and impact investing are the fastest growing categories for stewarding wealth. Investors around the world are making impact investments to unleash the power of capital for a greater good. As society and the financial industry move forward, a wider range of investment vehicles, as well as more diverse impact targets, will no doubt become available. Coupled with buyers making informed decisions about their acquisitions on the basis of where the profits from their purchases are going, people will be more and more able to direct their dollars to organizations they believe in or to people they want to see succeed. This means that tomorrow's wealth holders will be more confident in their assets and how they're being used and that these assets will be deployed with increasing efficiency.

WHAT IS THE MEANING OF WEALTH?

In the modern Western world, wealth has typically been seen as singular: the bottom line of one's bank account or the total dollars in one's investment portfolio. This is at least partially attributable to accounting, which has allowed people to measure wealth on a balance sheet. When wealth gets measured this way, it gets managed this way. Wealth can only move up or down; it becomes one-dimensional. Having adequate money to meet one's life goals is essential. Yet, the Specialization Age is naturally calling people to understand wealth as a more holistic concept.

There's already precedent for multidimensional wealth. In fact, for many, wealth has never been singular. Throughout history, as the dominating cultures focused on wealth in monetary terms, the cultures they dominated were forced to take an alternative approach. Communities that historically have been persecuted accumulate their wealth in different ways. For these people, it became necessary for wealth to be portable; for example, education is a key form of portable wealth. In fact, wealth has many facets, from the ecological wealth so integral to indigenous communities to the intellectual property that has become far more important as a store of wealth for business leaders.

Today's version of wealth seems to be moving closer to what people had in mind when they originally gave meaning to the word. Having a meaningful life contributes to being happy, and being happy may also contribute to making life more meaningful. For centuries, traditional wisdom has been that simply seeking pleasure for its own sake does not really make you happy in the long run. In fact, seeking wealth without meaning can be an unrewarding experience. Instead, when aspiring to a well-lived life, it might make more sense to look for things you find meaningful, like deep relationships, responsibility, and purposeful self-expression. When you do dedicate yourself to such worthy pursuits, chances are that you will also find pleasure—and happiness—along the way as abundance flows to you and back out into the universe again.

Wealth across the Ages

How has our relationship with wealth changed over time? And what might this relationship look like in the future? In exploring the evolution of wealth, I am attempting to answer these questions. Understanding this relationship as being pivotal to this book, my search delved into the fields of ancient history, business, economics, research, politics, and psychology. Rather than looking at wealth as a continuous part of history, let's look at some critical moments in time. Spoiler alert: what I found is that wealth is a looking glass that reflects cultures and society.

Wealth is an interesting word. It can mean very different things to different people. It dates back as far as the mid-thirteenth century from the Middle English *wele*, meaning 'well-being'; the Old English *wela* 'wealth' and in late Old English also 'welfare, well-being'; and the West Germanic *welon–*, 'to wish, well'.[1] If you were wondering if it's a coincidence that *health* and *wealth* sound like each other, it's not. If you take a look at *Webster's* and *MacMillan*, you'll find clues pointing to a dramatic change in the way the word wealth is used: from meaning "a sound, healthy, or prosperous state"[2] to "the state of being rich."[3]

In the time before money, wealth wasn't financial but sacred. This is still the case in some of today's indigenous communities, whose members see wealth as having an inherent value as opposed to being able to produce value. Around the sixth century BCE, coins emerged in Lydia, which is now a part of modern Turkey. The emergence of coinage made it much easier for the common people to become economic actors. Wealth was no longer the preserve of a small group: it could now be deconstructed, exchanged, and democratized. The empowering nature of wealth allowed individuals to have an impact on their world. However, note here, too, the shift from wealth being inherent to the individual to wealth being external to him or her—something to be acquired or not acquired, gained and lost, or never gotten at all.

The Buddha, Confucius, and Socrates were three of the most influential thinkers in human history. What's less well-known is that all three shaped people's relationship with and understanding of wealth. They ushered in the paradigm shift of rationality over superstition and belief. All three of these individuals were investigating what it means to be human. They all recognized that no one operates in isolation. It isn't that man is the measure of all things, but man's relationship with man is the measure of all things. The pursuit of wealth isn't a problem; the pursuit of wealth without virtue is.

The Renaissance was a rebirth of beauty and art, as well as the less celebrated birth of banking and brokerage. For the latter, 1602 was an important year, as it saw the first public share issuance or initial public offering take place, on behalf of the Dutch East India Company. This date also heralded a move away from feudalism to a new economic system: shareholder capitalism. Opportunities became so large that they couldn't be financed by an individual, so people got together to share the risk and reward. This led to a rapid expansion in the number of financial intermediaries, which quickly got out of hand.

The Renaissance was a rebirth of beauty and art, as well as the less celebrated birth of banking and brokerage.

Wealth was no longer controlled by its originators or owners but by their agents. This explosion of shareholder capitalism meant that owners became intermediated out of the system. Their agents' fiduciary duty became only a financial one. While these groups of shareholders (and, more to the point, their investments) led to a boom in the economy, no one asked the question, What do these groups of people have in common? The answer was nothing, other than a desire to make money.

People noticed that new wealth was being accumulated and there were new social problems to fix: whether the former development caused the latter is unclear, but the social problems could potentially be mitigated by the former. It's no coincidence that the birth of shareholder capitalism happened at the same time as the legal recognition of philanthropy, with philanthropy being defined as a model that encourages the private responsibility of the wealthy to give to the impoverished. Public oversight of this distribution of wealth ensures honesty on both sides of the transaction.

The first laws governing charity in the United Kingdom were written in 1601 under Queen Elizabeth I. Although wealth generation can easily lead the wealth generator to practice and even embrace disconnected individualism, others recognize that the people making up different elements or layers of society need to be much more interdependent. At the same time, common themes about wealth have emerged. By looking more closely at a few of these themes, we can see how people's relationship with wealth has changed and what it might become.

Although wealth generation can easily lead the wealth generator to practice and even embrace disconnected individualism, others recognize that the people making up different elements or layers of society need to be much more interdependent.

As I discussed earlier in the book, early concepts of wealth centered around stability—from sacred items born out of the earth, through durable property, to the holistic concept of well-being. Wealth was created and stewarded over lifetimes and across generations. Finance enabled wealth to reach around the world. British trust law emerged in the twelfth century to allow a wealthy noble to keep his property safe while he left to lend his sword to the Crusades.

Within a century, debt was being traded in Venice, then throughout Europe; this was followed by trading in equity. The noble could now stay at home while his money traveled. As finance became increasingly intermediated, the distance between a wealth holder and his or her wealth has stretched to the point where today we have little concept of being connected to the numbers that appear on bank and brokerage statements. Capitalism has accelerated the creation of opportunities to generate wealth. Among the first true capitalists were equity investors.

In the United Kingdom, these included investors in the East India Company, a competitor to the world's first listed business. From London's docks, investors would wave farewell to the ship they had funded; they would then wait two years for the boat to return so they could discover whether their investment had paid off. This is where the phrase "my ship came in" comes from. The modern shareholder works on a very different timescale. By way of illustration, the typical holding period of a share has fallen from around eight years in 1960 to six months in 2010.[4]

From these measurements in years, today's trading now deals in microseconds. This is possible because all the pieces of the financial system, where our wealth sits, are now incredibly well connected, with trades being made swiftly over super-high-speed fiber optic networks. At the same time, investors themselves often feel disconnected from the financial system due to its overcomplexity, which leads to a lack of clarity. Encouragingly, a push for transparency in the system is being driven by the next generation of wealth holders, who are being aided by technology such as social media and big data. Clarity is also starting to be offered by companies with new investment opportunities and forward-thinking leaders who are aware and willing to share information about their companies' total exposure to liabilities like product liability, contractual liability, and advertising liability, as well as footprint and impact.

From these measurements in years, today's trading now deals in microseconds.

One of the things I particularly like about the strategies I use at my firm, Centric Capital Advisors, is that they are transparent: my clients are able to see what I am trading and when I am trading. That's not always the case in the industry. For example, when a traditional financial firm manages an investor's hedge fund or another super-sophisticated investment vehicle, it sends you a statement once a month. These firms are usually doing a good job, and it is a complex set of tasks they are managing day to day and second to second, but that lack of transparency and clarity for the investor is not a good thing. The financial house of cards came down in 2008 in part due to lack of transparency. People didn't even know what they were buying; if they had, they may have asked for more accountability from their advisors' industry. Sometimes I call what I do an *open-source hedge fund*. I use complex strategies, but you can see into them. You know what you own all the time.

At the core of finance is a paradox: money isn't actually worth anything. Money's value is entirely symbolic, sustained by convention and a pervasive social latticework of trust. Trust is the cornerstone of the financial system, and it can be seen in the history of many words still in use: for example, the term *credit* can be traced back to the Latin *credo*. Before the banking system existed, wealth was stored in physical, tangible objects such as gold, coins, and even land; investments; and loans given to merchants or young politicians, all of which had important symbolic value. Once banking emerged, paper and metal currencies became symbolic placeholders of value, built only on trust.

The financial house of cards came down in 2008 in part due to lack of transparency.

By the twentieth century, pride in wealth was all-consuming. With increasing variety in clothes, food, and household items, shopping became an important cultural activity. Combined with planned obsolescence and advertising to increase consumer spending, these factors created a perfect storm of consumerism. In 1899, Thorstein Veblen coined the term *conspicuous consumption* to describe the ostentatious display of wealth. While it was originally seen as distasteful, such ostentation is becoming even less socially acceptable given large and visible wealth disparities prevalent in modern society. At the same time, it can sometimes be a struggle to see wealth, which is typically hidden within the financial system.

Given that the financial industry is fueled by something that exists only through trust, it's ironic that international consumer polls show it to be the least trusted industry. The damage from the global financial crisis of 2008 wasn't just monetary: it destroyed the credibility of the sector. The federal government has tried to step in, using regulation to restore trust. The unintentional consequence is that, as a society, we've lost the sense of what is right. Markets outsourced their sense of morality to the regulator and their social responsibility to the government.

From its current low ebb, trust will slowly return. The government is unlikely to be the most influential factor in restoring trust. Technology could play that role, however. By enabling open communication, peer-to-peer reviews, social media, and the emergence of innovations such as blockchain, technology is putting trust at the heart of interactions. When this trust is shared among new cultures and new wealth holders, we should see improved well-being in the ecosystem of wealth.

Glossary

401(k): A retirement plan that is sponsored by an employer. The employee's contribution to the plan is taken out of his or her pretax income. Some employers will match the employee's contribution up to a certain amount.

529 plan: A state-sponsored account allowing individuals and families to save for educational expenses. Most states offer 529 plans, and some states offer tax advantages to residents using them. If the earnings are used for college expenses, they're not taxed.

asset management: The professional management by a financial services company of a client's investments. The investments can include securities, such as stocks, bonds, and mutual funds, and tangible assets, such as real estate.

atlas client: A person who is self-empowered to create the financial experience he or she desires in the Specialization Age.

atlas shift: The moment in time when the Information Age tipped the financial services landscape into being so complicated that investors needed to partner with a new kind of advisor to manage it and to take on more personal responsibility for creating their desired financial experience.

CFP®: A CERTIFIED FINANCIAL PLANNER™. A CFP® is a professional who has earned certification from the CFP® Board. Such certification requires extensive training and experience, as well as adherence to high ethical standards.

commission: The money that a broker or advisor charges a client for advice and handling of financial accounts.

estate planning: Making decisions about how one's estate or wealth will be distributed following one's death and setting up the estate so those decisions are properly carried out.

fee-based financial advisor: A financial advisor compensated by a combination of fees charged to the client for financial planning and commissions earned by selling financial products to the client.

fee-only financial advisor: A financial advisor paid directly by his or her client. No compensation is contingent upon the purchase or sale of a financial product.

fiduciary: A trustee who is legally appointed to hold assets for someone. He or she manages the assets for the other person's benefit versus his or her own.

financial experience: The direct observation of or participation in past financial events as a basis of knowledge and awareness moving forward.

financial experience advisor: A financial professional who inspires confidence in his or her clients by leveraging his or her alliance partner network and key wealth-building strategies to create a truly unique financial experience that is personalized to the individual client's situation and desired outcomes.

FINRA: Financial Industry Regulatory Authority. FINRA was created in July 2007 when the National Association of Securities Dealers and the New York Stock Exchange's regulation committee merged. This regulatory body governs business between brokers, dealers, and the public. FINRA is the largest regulatory body (that's not associated with the government) of US securities firms.

holistic life planning: An approach to financial planning that takes into account that everyone has their own unique sets of needs and best solutions, and each aspect of a family's personal finances needs to be considered both on its own and in how changes in that one place will impact every other aspect of the family's finances and life. A financial advisor using this very important approach considers how the varied aspects of financial well-being are intertwined—and how they should work together—to help a client achieve his or her financial goals.

Information Age: A historic period beginning in the late twentieth century characterized by the rapid shift from traditional industry based on industrialization to an economy predicated on the fact that information is a commodity that can be quickly and widely disseminated and is easily available, especially through the use of computer technology.

net worth: Liabilities subtracted from assets. Liabilities can include mortgages, loans, credit card debt, and more. Assets can include investments, real estate, savings, personal property, and more.

portfolio: The mix of investment instruments owned by an investor. A portfolio can be composed of bonds, common stocks, preferred stocks, and other securities. Portfolios can be managed by financial professionals or held by investors.

RIA: Registered Investment Advisor. The Investment Advisers Act of 1940 defined an RIA as a "person or firm that, for compensation, is engaged in the act of providing advice, making recommendations, issuing reports or furnishing analyses on securities, either directly or through publications."[1] An RIA is registered with state investment authorities or the SEC.

Specialization Age: The period following the Information Age, characterized by the demand for customization in everything from the presentation of information to products and services. This demand for customization is driving innovations that apply this principle to new and different frontiers. The arts and sciences of this age will be defined by those who intelligently filter information according to what's valuable to them. This sets up a situation where a person knows what he or she wants in life and has access to the information necessary to pursue it but needs advice and specialization tools to effectively filter the information and be enabled to pursue those values.

traditional financial advisor: An advisor who provides financial advice to clients and is compensated in return. Financial planners, investment managers, and those who sell financial products can all be traditional financial advisors.

wirehouse: A term used to describe a broker-dealer. Modern-day wirehouses range from small regional brokerages to large institutions with global footprints. The national firms Morgan Stanley, Merrill Lynch, UBS and Wells Fargo are thought of most commonly. The term was coined when brokerage firms were connected to their branches primarily through private telephone and telegraph wires.

Acknowledgments

I thank Svetlana Rassman, Suzanne Murray, Benjamin Castillo, L. Williamson, Roger Davis, Jake Pfeiffer, Gopher Rassman, Thomas J. Collins Jr., Thomas J. Collins Sr., John Egan, Merry Rassman, Rod Rassman, William H. Mobeck, Mitchell Rassman, Dusty Farber, Chris and Gary Collins, Kareem Masarni, Christopher Hynes, Kyle Quinn, Mary Mobeck, Tom Lemons, Frank Acosta, Kyle Filipowicz, Brian Conlan, M. J. Dugan, Benjamin College, Dan Moore, Rob Pierce, and Phillip Mannix. The majority of the list is unwritten because the people who have inspired me to write this book I have not yet met, but they will understand me through my words and my work. I am convinced my best mentor, my best client, my closest friends, and my biggest fans are either around me or I have yet to meet them. *There is no end to our becoming.*

About the Author

William Rassman, CFP®, is a Certified Financial Planner™ practitioner for successful families and individuals, as well as an accomplished speaker and author. He is a Partner and Director of Advisory Services at Centric Capital Advisors, and he began his career at Smith Barney in the financial district of New York in 2008.

Will graduated from Wagner College in New York, New York, with a BA in economics. A former college hockey player and NCAA golfer, Will lives in Manhattan Beach, California, with his wife, Svetlana. He is an active member of the Financial Planning Association, the Santa Monica Chamber of Commerce, and Toastmasters International. During his free time, he enjoys volunteering with his dog, Gopher.

Endnotes

INTRODUCTION

1. Atsma, Aaron J. 2000. "Atlas." *Theoi Project.* Accessed September 26, 2018. http://www.theoi.com/Titan/TitanAtlas.html.

Definition of *atlas*

2. *Merriam-Webster,* s.v. "atlas." Accessed September 14, 2018. https://www.merriam-webster.com/dictionary/atlas.

CHAPTER 1

1. Whelan, Kelly. n.d. "How the Weekend Was Won: History Lesson—How the 8 Hour Day Was Won." *The Livelyhood Journey* (blog). Accessed October 26, 2018. http://www.pbs.org/livelyhood/workday/weekend/8hourday.html.
2. Rosen, David. 2017. "What Happened to the 40-Hour Workweek?" *Counterpunch Magazine,* December 29, 2017. https://www.counterpunch.org/2017/12/29/what-happened-to-the-40-hour-workweek/.
3. Saad, Lydia. 2014. "The '40-Hour' Workweek Is Actually Longer—By 7 Hours." Gallup (website), August 29, 2014. https://news.gallup.com/poll/175286/hour-workweek-actually-longer-seven-hours.aspx.
4. Ferriss, Tim, and Derek Sivers. 2015. "Derek Sivers: Interviews → Tim Ferriss Show: Part 2." *The Tim Ferriss Show,* December 28, 2015. https://sivers.org/2015-12-ferriss2.
5. McSpadden, Kevin. 2015. "You Now Have a Shorter Attention Span than a Goldfish." *TIME,* May 14, 2015. http://www.time.com/3858309/attention-spans-goldfish.

CHAPTER 2

1. Strom, Stephanie. 2009. "Elie Weisel Levels Scorn at Madoff." *New York Times*, February 26, 2009. https://www.nytimes.com/2009/02/27/business/27madoff.html.
2. Hamel, Gary, and Michele Zanini. 2017. "What We Learned about Bureaucracy from 7,000 HBR Readers." *Harvard Business Review*, August 10, 2017. https://hbr.org/2017/08/what-we-learned-about-bureaucracy-from-7000-hbr-readers.

CHAPTER 3

1. Tobin Investment Planning LLC. n.d. "Benefits of an Independent Registered Investment Advisor." Accessed December 5, 2018. http://tobininvestmentplanning.com/ria/ria/
2. Kaplan Financial Education. 2018. "What Does a CFP® Professional Do?" October 23, 2018. https://www.kaplanfinancial.com/resources/cfp/what-does-a-cfp-professional-do/.
3. Investopedia. n.d. "Certified Financial Planner – CFP." Accessed October 17, 2018. https://www.investopedia.com/terms/c/cfp.asp.
4. Nike. 2018. "Nike by You." Accessed December 2, 2018. https://www.nike.com/us/en_us/c/nikeid.
5. Reebok. 2018. "Make It Your Own." Accessed December 2, 2018. https://www.reebok.com/us/customize.
6. Center for Foot Care. n.d. "Is It Normal to Have Different-Sized Feet?" Accessed September 12, 2018. https://cincinnatifootcare.com/normal-different-sized-feet/.
7. Geewax, Marilyn. 2015. "The Tipping Point: Most Americans No Longer Are Middle Class." *The Two-Way* (blog), NPR, December 9, 2015. https://www.npr.org/sections/thetwo-way/2015/12/09/459087477/the-tipping-point-most-americans-no-longer-are-middle-class.
8. Novotney, Amy. 2009. "The Price of Affluence: New Research Shows that Privileged Teens May Be More Self-Centered—and Depressed—than Ever Before." *Monitor on Psychology* 40, No. 1. http://www.apa.org/monitor/2009/01/teens.aspx.
9. MacMillan, Amanda. 2011. "People in Affluent Nations May Be More

Depression-Prone." CNN, July 26, 2011. http://www.cnn.com/2011/HEALTH/07/26/affluent.depression.prone/index.html.

10. Rector, Robert. 2007. "How Poor Are America's Poor? Examining the 'Plague' of Poverty in America." The Heritage Foundation, August 27, 2007. https://www.heritage.org/poverty-and-inequality/report/how-poor-are-americas-poor-examining-the-plague-poverty-america.

CHAPTER 4

1. Dale, Stephen. 2018. "Heuristics and Biases—The Science of Decision Making." *Communities & Collaboration* (blog), July 29, 2018. http://www.stephendale.com/2018/07/29/heuristics-and-biases-the-science-of-decision-making.
2. Investopedia. n.d. "Behavioral Finance." Accessed September 13, 2018. https://www.investopedia.com/terms/b/behavioralfinance.asp.
3. Marquit, Miranda. 2018. "What Is Behavioral Finance?" Investor Junkie, August 22, 2018. https://investorjunkie.com/24423/behavioral-finance/.
4. Cormier, Warren. 2015. "What Is Behavioral Finance—And Why Do We Need It?" American Society of Pension Professionals & Actuaries, September 4, 2015. https://www.asppa.org/news-resources/browse-topics/what-behavioral-finance-—-and-why-do-we-need-it.
5. Investopedia, "Behavioral Finance."

CHAPTER 5

1. Hamer, Ashley. 2017. "Loss Aversion Says that the Pain of Loss Is Stronger than the Joy of Gain." Curiosity, January 27, 2017. https://curiosity.com/topics/loss-aversion-says-that-the-pain-of-loss-is-stronger-than-the-joy-of-gain-curiosity.
2. Davis, Roger. 2016. *Wall Street's Just Not that Into You: An Insider's Guide to Protecting and Growing Wealth.* New York, NY: Routledge.

CHAPTER 6

1. Elkins, Kathleen. 2017. "A Brief History of the 401(k), which Changed

How Americans Retire." CNBC, January 4, 2017. https://www.cnbc.com/2017/01/04/a-brief-history-of-the-401k-which-changed-how-americans-retire.html.

2. American Association for Long-Term Care Insurance. 2018. "Long-Term Care Insurance Policy Costs—2018." Accessed October 14, 2018. http://www.aaltci.org/long-term-care-insurance/learning-center/ltcfacts.php.

CHAPTER 7

1. Pesce, Nicole Lyn. 2017. "People Exchanged $17.6 Billion on Venmo Last Year, Because Emoji." Moneyish, April 28, 2017. https://www.marketwatch.com/story/people-exchanged-176-billion-on-venmo-last-year-because-emoji-2017-04-28-10884541.
2. Woodward, Kevin. 2018. "A Consumer Survey Yields More Indications that Zelle Is Catching Up to Venmo." Digital Transactions, June 20, 2018. https://www.digitaltransactions.net/a-consumer-survey-yields-more-indications-that-zelle-is-catching-up-to-venmo/.

CHAPTER 8

1. MacBride, Elizabeth. 2016. "The Longevity Paradox: As Americans Live Longer, They Run the Risk of Outliving Their Money." *InvestmentNews*, August 22, 2016. https://www.investmentnews.com/article/20160822/FEATURE/160809926/the-longevity-paradox-as-americans-live-longer-they-run-the-risk-of.
2. Ferriss, Tim, and Art De Vany. 2018. "The Tim Ferriss Show Transcripts: Art De Vany." *The Tim Ferriss Show*, June 1, 2018. https://tim.blog/2018/06/01/the-tim-ferriss-show-transcripts-art-de-vany/.
3. MacBride, "The Longevity Paradox."
4. University of Southern California, Master of Arts in Gerontology and Master of Aging Services Management Programs. n.d. "Infographics: Americans Are Living Longer." Accessed October 15, 2018. https://gerontology.usc.edu/resources/infographics/americans-are-living-longer/.
5. Trustees of the Social Security and Medicare Trust Funds. 2018.

"A Summary of the 2018 Annual Reports." Social Security Administration. https://www.ssa.gov/oact/TRSUM/.

6. CBS News. 2016. "Cruise Ship Living: Retiring to a Life at Sea." August 22, 2016. https://www.cbsnews.com/news/cruise-ship-living-retiring-to-a-life-at-sea/.
7. Buettner, Dan. 2016. "Power 9®." Blue Zones, November 10, 2016. https://www.bluezones.com/2016/11/power-9/.
8. Yotopoulos, Amy, and Jonathan Streeter. 2016. "Social Portfolios Are Just as Important as Financial Portfolios." Stanford Center on Longevity. http://longevity.stanford.edu/2016/11/09/social-portfolios-are-just-as-important-as-financial-portfolios/.

CHAPTER 9

1. Baker, Maverick. 2018. "How to Eliminate Plastic Waste and Plastic Pollution with Science and Engineering." Interesting Engineering, August 16, 2018. https://interestingengineering.com/how-to-eliminate-plastic-waste-and-plastic-pollution-with-science-and-engineering.

BONUS CHAPTER

1. Luminous Words, s.v. "Wealth: Etymology." Accessed September 14, 2018. http://luminouswords.net/wealth/.
2. *Merriam-Webster,* s.v. "weal." Accessed October 14, 2018. https://www.merriam-webster.com/dictionary/weal.
3. *Macmillan Dictionary,* s.v. "wealth." Accessed October 14, 2018. https://www.macmillandictionary.com/us/dictionary/american/wealth.
4. Harding, Sy. 2011. "Stock Market Becomes Short Attention Span Theater of Trading." *Forbes*, January 21, 2011. https://www.forbes.com/sites/greatspeculations/2011/01/21/stock-market-becomes-short-attention-span-theater-of-trading/

GLOSSARY

1. Investment Advisors Act of 1940, 54 Stat. 847, 15 U.S.C. 80b-1–80b-2 (1940).

Made in the USA
San Bernardino, CA
29 January 2019